When Will Civilization Arrive?

BY ROBERT E. BARR

DORRANCE
PUBLISHING CO
EST. 1920
PITTSBURGH, PENNSYLVANIA 15238

Dorrance Publishing Co
585 Alpha Drive
Pittsburgh, PA 15238
Visit our website at *www.dorrancebookstore.com*

ISBN: 978-1-6470-2521-2
eISBN: 978-1-6470-2695-0

When Will Civilization Arrive?

Table of Contents

Prologue

History revealed the Romans produced and evolved a working civilization whereby the Empire could survive. Certainly, the Empire was not a utopia, but there was an order to the populace and proletariat comprised of business owners and laborers, low-level workers, and, unfortunately, slaves. Initially, the empire grew, prospered, and traded with distant kingdoms. While time and progress are not the culprits, Roman leaders allowed themselves the luxury of selfish, greedy, and controlling introverted thinking. For the supreme leaders, sovereignty, greatness, and mostly government for the good of the proletariat became greatly diminished goals. Emperors, senators, and the elite began showing increased traits toward wealth, control, power, and a quest for personal pleasures, which they deemed well deserved. Late in the life of the Empire, Rome succumbed and was overtaken because of a lack of nationalistic thinking, an increase in self-indulgent people, decreases in morality, and the ever-expanding drug use were factors in a non-recoverable death spiral for the Roman Empire. Can we place America somewhere on an analogous track with the Romans? It appears many factors of the Roman demise fit the US history puzzle, whereby our civilization may not possess sufficient leadership.

Acknowledgments

The illustrations of Shannon Fausey bring a new dimension to imagination and idea perception. Her attention to detail elicits more than the drawing, but awareness and a transference to the situation are elicited. Her clarity of description is proportional to talent working in time.

The letter donated by Shannon Fausey was received by Lilla Downey, the mother of Johnny Downey, who was killed by a landmine in Vietnam on September 11, 1969. Shannon was Johnny's sister-in-law. The letter was written by Captain John E. Borton, commander of Field Artillery, 3rd Battalion, 6th Artillery. Captain Borton was sorry and most sincere, and regretfully, the letter to Mrs. Downey was not a singular case. By the Vietnam War end, 58,220 names were on the Vietnam Memorial wall, but passage of time has added 100 more names.

From commanders to branch headquarters, letters were written to mothers and fathers who prayed to never receive any such death letter, but as destiny would have its way; letters were written and mailed or delivered by the thousands – remorsefully. As in other wars and conflicts, regret and sorrow are without measure – or, reward. The untimely departure of another human being and their potential contributions to humanity are what we must live without.

Chapter 1
BEGINNINGS

From the distant past, Homo sapiens ancestors diverted from a lineage 6.2 million to 4.6 million ago years from present. Humanoids did not descend from apes or chimpanzees. Somewhere near 300,000 years before present modern looking humans began to appear, and the passing of another quarter million years or so produced rudimentary human behaviors. Between two million years to a half million years ago, fire and cooking became humanoid favorites.

Consistency in human records is progressing but elusive, since paleoanthropology and archaeology and other sciences have continued to add new findings to the humanoid trail for some time. Anthropology and paleoanthropology have regarded initial tool making to be contained in the Pleistocene epoch of 2.58 million years ago to 11,700 years ago, but tools have been found in the lake, Turkama area that date approximately 3.3 million years ago, the middle of the Pliocene era, 5.3 million years ago to 2.58 million years ago. The question prevails: did Australopithecus have tools? Could the rudimentary beginning of civilization begin earlier than present thinking and evidence?

Probably not. But we must keep open minds. The millions of years before present contain some surprises, but as early humanoids transitioned to the Pleistocene Epoch, Old Stone Age, inventiveness and toolmaking progressed. Maybe, humanoids could get a better chance near fertile areas surrounding the Mediterranean.

If the world is to possess civilization, it must start in early fertile areas. Fossil records are indicative that the eastern coast of the Mediterranean, in the Levant, a region NNE to SSE of the coast, had rudimentary civilization. Over 13,000 years BC or well over 15,000 years ago the Natufian culture existed in the Levant to a degree where some or more citizens could remain entrenched. They were not migratory as were preceding clans. Culture was sophisticated enough for some to have fixed habitats, maybe a trade.

Drawing from the many definitions of civilizations, several factors prevail: language, writing, historic buildings, rules, and auspices of science. In some form, laborers or service class people have a niche as well as the elite and rulers. Of course, the picture is not complete. The laborers, for example, might procure building materials and sufficient agriculture to support that portion of a beginning society which are not self-sufficient but are societal rule makers or process the early makings of money.

Early on, however, quasi-cultures were inadvertently moving toward civilized society. Possibly, from Natufian gatherings or small communities, Neolithic populations or settlements may have been the first at organized living – beginnings of civilization. For a continuance of food, Shubayqa, in the Levant, may have possessed the oldest evidence of bread making capability. The site shows a date between 14,000 and 15,000 years ago. Such capability gives evidence for supporting non-laboring middle-class people.

History is replete with humanities attempting civilization through territorial control, power, and wealth. But can a real civilization be achieved through war? Probably, any answer is arguable, yet various past world conquerors might argue war is truly the path to civilization. Clans, cave dwellers, Cro-Magnons, Neanderthals, and, remotely, Australopithecines of prehistory must have had disputes over hunting and living territories. In prehistory times, war was extremely remote or nonexistent, since forethought, planning, and killing weapons would have been required in clans or tribes more interested in surviving the moment. For the early hominid, concepts of civilization must wait a couple of million years.

Fortunately, for modern humans, the coexistence with Smilodon, saber tooth tiger, woolly mammoths, and woolly rhinoceroses was the occupation of Cro-Magnons or Neanderthals. Daily survival was prime motivation for these hominids in the Pleistocene. Clans or tribes were the societal gatherings, maybe in caves, but organized war leading to civilization was thousands of years away.

From the best interpretation of fossil records, Neanderthals, became extinct about 40,000 years ago, but probably not by the hands of Cro-Magnons. However, they left us about 2.5 percent of their DNA, possibly a little more. Reasons vary for the continuance of Cro-Magnons and the disappearance of Neanderthals, who survived for 360,000 years or more. What happened? Absolute answers are not available. Wars are highly unlikely, but fossil records indicate Cro-Magnon was quite adaptable to earthly changes. Ingenuity for making tighter fitting clothes and footwear for glacier conditions pushed survival. With the onslaught of the last Ice Age ending some 12,000 years ago, Cro-Magnons were the surviving hominids while Neanderthals went extinct 28,000 years before. Cro-Magnons are or became us.

In terms of war, conquering, and civilization, Rome and the Roman Empire have a significant place in humanity's quest for civilization. Rome had insignificant beginnings as early as the eighth century BC, but Rome became a world empire from 27 BC to 476 AD. For times before Christ, during, and long after Christ, Rome was the world power. Civilization carries some manifestations: architecture, engineering, art, literature, technology, law, a form of religion, and warfare for expansion, which Rome craved. Rome expansion was vast to include: portions of West and South Europe, Balkans, Middle East, Egypt, Levant, Arabia, north African coast, part of Mesopotamia, and Italy.

For the better part of 500 years, the Roman Empire had a grasp on civilization, but it slipped away quite surely on the shoulders of corrupt leaders. Self-indulgent senatorial thinking over sovereign, national preservation forethought cost the Emperor and leaders their country. Corruption arrives through self-indulgent pleasures, drugs, immortality, lawlessness, and a lack of religion. Within the Roman Empire, ideas of continued nationality and advancing greatness of Empire were on the decline or nonexistent. Although the Roman Empire had committed warfare on other countries and dominions for years, its last weak, introspective years allowed Attila the Hun to successfully invade the Eastern Roman empire.

It seemed Romans had given history a precursor and blueprint of a civilized nation's steady build up and decline to a complete collapse. It allowed the fundamental building principles to crumble before corruption, immortality, self-indulgence, and godless ideals. Rome lost its ethics for civilization and leadership. These same ethics containing, at least, honesty and responsibility should be characteristics of national citizens inculcated by family and education. Rome lost these ideals and, worse, a hold on civilization.

Chapter 2
THE GREAT FLOOD

According to biblical scholars, the Great Flood or Deluge happened around 2,348 BC or some 4,367 years ago, and was good for world coverage. Modern scientists dispute the world coverage idea, and other studies have dated Noah's flood to a determination of 8,400 years BP. This time would probably support the Mediterranean flood over the Bosporus into the Black Sea.

The beginnings of the Great Flood started much earlier than the quasi-date of 8,400 years BP. Melting from Earth's last glaciation may have started around 20,000 to 18,000 years ago. Of course, the meltwater had to go somewhere, and the North Sea may have been a target. Meanwhile, the freshwater Black Sea was losing water and finally lost enough that the Sea of Azov became dry. The decrease in Black Sea water level was several hundred feet below the Mediterranean, and the separating dry land feature was the Bosporus. Eventually, the water level differences were overpowering for the Bosporus, and an unfathomable amount of Mediterranean Sea water deluged the freshwater Black Sea. A great flood occurred.

Catastrophic events would have occurred for prehistoric villages and settlements in what will be Eastern Europe, northern parts of what is now Turkey, and southwestern lands of the current Soviet Union. If the latest Bosporus collapsed date of 7,200 to 8,400 years BP is correct, then, the flood was in the early Holocene Epoch and followed the Younger Dryas, 12,900 to 11,700 years BP, which was a time of rapid cooling after the past great glaciation began melting about 20,000 to 18,000 years ago. The opposites of climes were upon the Earth. Causes for the Younger Dryas vary, but a North Atlantic cessation of the warmer southern salt water conveyor current that lasted for, maybe, 1,200 years seems likely.

Settlements established around the Black Sea lower water levels shores were subjected to glaciation, melting, a Younger Dryas cooling, and a final melting to fill the Black Sea with salt water. Probably, from the beginning Younger Dryas onset to the flood, beginnings of cultures or any stabilized communities experienced some rough, precarious times.

From what science and geology reveals, melting glaciation from the late Pleistocene Epoch to the early Holocene Epoch has been the cause of flooding. The stories of Noah are generally based on Mesopotamian writings that deal with the beginnings of time. With the best offerings of science, current scientists do not place earthly beginnings anywhere near the flood but about 4.6 billion years in the past – quite a difference.

However, Noah's story is closely related to Utnapishtim in the Epic of Gilgamesh. Utnapishtim's and Noah's arks were similar, and the few Mesopotamian tablets strike similarities. Possibly, the ark inception occurred in Mesopotamia or the present Iraq. Noah may have floated an ark in the Black Sea, but the Earth was probably not covered with the flood. There are at least two religious reasons God sent the flood. The Atra-Hasis version is synopsized for God to reduce the Earth's overpopulation. Secondarily, the Hebrew version of God's flood was to punish humans for their sin and wickedness.

For the religious version of Noah, rain occurred for 40 days and nights. In all probability, the equalization of seawater from the Mediterranean to the Black Sea through the Bosporus lasted 300 days or more. As the Black Sea filled, it's east – west water would have stretched over 700 miles with the shortest distance between two points being 150 miles as the Black Sea basin filled. Noah reportedly could not see any shores. If Noah was theoretically 30 feet above the sea in the ark, his line of sight distance would be approximately 9.5 miles, and if he was 40 feet above the sea surface, his line of sight distance would be about 11 miles. With a distance of greater than 20 miles from Black Sea shores, Noah could not see them.

Noah landed on Mount Ararat after150 days of ark floating. There was no power, since Noah had no destination, except survival. If any current was in the Black Sea, it was coming from the Mediterranean through the Bosporus to the northeast; otherwise, the ark was adrift. Mount Ararat is approximately 350 miles from the closest Black Sea shore, which indicates Noah's landing preceded a fair receding of the sea since his Mount Ararat encounter. While the flood date remains in question, scientists and paleontologists are fairly certain the flood was not world extensive. In ancient writings of history, there were often cultural heroes who could save the world or correct the wrongs. Is it possible Noah was such a hero?

One hundred thousand years before present, BP, Mesopotamia and the Great Oasis, contained settlements, but when glaciers began to melt 20,000 years ago, lakes and seas began to form. The Bosporus Strait could hold the Mediterranean waters back just so long. Water forces broke through, and people in the Mesopotamian areas had to seek higher ground of which science has remains. Civilization was not present, but settlements were showing cultural signs. Settlement inhabitants certainly did not wish to lose huts, blankets, weapons, or food as the basin's brackish layer arose from waters pouring through the Bosporus Strait to form the Black Sea.

Prior to 20,000 BP, the world sea levels were much lower, but as the melting began, ice waters went into oceans and filled the ancient Lake Agassiz shallow basin in what is now Central North America. Lake Agassiz was larger than the Great Lakes combined. The prehistoric River Warren was probably responsible for draining Lake Agassiz from 12,000 to 9,000 years ago. The prehistoric lake is responsible for forming many lakes in Canada and the northern US. Much later, civilizations were to tap into these glacial waters, since the subsequent lakes formed have lasted several thousand years.

The Great Lakes or Laurentian Great Lakes probably began filling from retreating glacier melt water about 14,000 years ago with the glaciers forming the Great Lakes' basins upon advancing and retreating. Much melt water was left behind, enough for 21 percent of the world's freshwater. The Saint Lawrence River is technically a seaway connecting the Great Lakes to the Atlantic Ocean, and the best data indicates the Saint Lawrence River was formed about 10,000 years ago. To some degree, southern bodies of water correlate to greater ages than those farther north.

Lake Agassiz, the Great Lakes, and glacial melting were in various melting or forming processes before or around Noah's Ark time. Of course, absolute knowledge of this is impossible. Since the Black Sea was filling, glacier melt was a contributing factor, and as the Black Sea filled, settlements and people were forced to move higher or away. From Noah's viewpoint, the situation in the world looked bleak. However, many thousands of miles to the northwest, glaciers were melting, basins were being formed, and many fresh water lakes were being formed, but the Earth was not covered with water. While various forms of life may have been existent on the ark, many forms of life were on Earth's dry land parts.

Ancient Great Flood writings describe Noah, his family, and animals as the only survivors upon the Earth. Apparently, all else had been destroyed, and for all that Noah could perceive, the catastrophic happening indicated complete annihilation. Within a broad span of time, Cro-Magnons coexisted with Neanderthals from about 100,000 years ago to around 40,000 years ago, and Cro-Magnons in Europe blended with Homo sapiens. Essentially, Cro-Magnons are Homo sapiens. If the world had been covered with water, early or late Homo would not have survived. We are Homo sapiens, and from Homo sapiens, modern ideas, innovations, societies, and, possibly, civilizations were derived.

Chapter 3
ANCIENT EGYPTIANS

When considering civilizations, the Egyptians must be considered major contributors to the progress of humanity. Archaeological knowledge indicates the first pyramid, Saqqara, during the reign of Pharaoh Djoser was built between 2,630 BC and 2,610 BC or more than 4,600 years ago. Before the building, a preface of organized stability was required. A magnanimous undertaking required organization, cooperation, higher orders of thought, engineering, architectural skills, thousands of laborers, and immeasurable logistics, which is difficult in retrospect to imagine. In terms of modern thinking and heavy equipment, it is difficult to conceive of or undertake such a project, and we are quite aware the Egyptians possessed no heavy lifting equipment. To serve the Pharaoh to the ultimate degree, some form of civilization necessarily existed.

More recent excavations have increased pyramid findings to a probable 138. Estimates of construction years range from 2,670 BC to 664 BC, a spread of over two millennia. For the Egyptians or culture to have obtained and retained capabilities to construct such a number of pyramids is indicative of a workable, purposeful civilization. A favorite area for building of pyramids was the Giza Plateau, and here are the exemplary pyramids of Menkaure, Khafre, and Khufu. Of the pyramids at Giza, the Great Pyramid of Khufu generates the most mystery and curiosity for archaeologists and scholars of antiquity.

Many archaeologists have added enlightenment to building of the pyramids, especially those at Giza. Pierre Tallet and Mark Lehner have contributed recent knowledge that fills many knowledge gaps of Egyptian pyramid construction. miraculous finds of papyri records at Wadi al-Jarf provided knowledge hereto unknown. The Papyrus scrolls, unmolested for thousands of years, included a journal of Merer, a head overseer for Pharaoh Khufu. However, it should be noted that Hemiunu was Vizier and architect of Khufu's pyramid. Apparently, after Khufu's pyramid was finished near his death at 27 years of reign, plans, drawings, and Merer's journal were no longer necessary, but they deserved a place of safety and obscurity to preserve Egyptian secrecy. The caves of Wadi al-Jarf along the Red Sea coast were the epitome of secrecy and obscurity. The ancient journals of Merer contained his wisdom and those from thousands of years before. Similarly, for copper tools used for building the pyramids, Wadi al-Jarf provided an ancient harbor on the Red Sea where the tools and boats were stored in caves. The Wadi al-Jarf caves provided nearly indefinite security since the Red Sea was not always navigable and the caves were obscure.

The Giza Pyramids required sailing abilities of Egyptian builders not normally emphasized by Egyptian historians, but ports on the Mediterranean Sea were needed for food procurement. Red Sea sailing supplied copper, while Nile sailing provided transport of necessary pyramid building stones. Best estimates are that the great pyramid was begun in a little more than 4,600 years ago, and for such a project, supply canals were probably built from the Nile to near the Giza Pyramids. After build completion the canals were undoubtedly covered and camouflaged. Weather, wind, sand, and time completed the camouflage job. Mark Lehner, director of Ancient Egypt Research Associates, indicated that as the Nile flooded, stones could be delivered to Giza through a system of canals and harbors. Builders of the Giza Pyramids were astute enough to know floating 2.5 tons stones on the Nile was infinitely better than sand dragging them for miles. Then, from the Nile, canals made stone positioning easier near Giza. Most stones for Khufu's pyramid weigh in the 2.5-ton range, but the King's chamber contains stones from 25 to 80 tons. From quarry to near Giza, sailing was undoubtedly the method, maybe, the only reasonable way. The distance from Aswan to Giza is about 500 miles. Imagination is tasked for visions of land transportation of an 80-ton stone.

If Egyptian archaeologists can assemble an edifice as large and impressive as Khufu's pyramid and orient it to true North within parameters less than an inch, it seems quite feasible they were knowledgeable of levers and fulcrums. Stones arrived by boats on the Nile and were rerouted to canals. Levers unloaded stones to wooden sleds, which were pulled and pushed with water in front to reduced sand friction. Water quantity must be just right. Possibly, the stone was levered again to a ramp, which transitioned to a series of positioning levers.

Getting the pyramidion on the top of the pyramid undoubtedly took a series of polished slides, a combination of levers and fulcrums, ropes, and at least a hundred laborers not being counterproductive. Once the Pyramidion was in place, anchors, ropes, planks, pivotal points, or other evidence were removed, which may have taken years.

Many theorists propose Egyptians did not possess the knowledge, expertise, or engineering skills to have built as many as 138 pyramids or engineered 65 tombs in the Valley of the Kings. Realizing the engineering and labor required at this number is nudging the impossible. Narrowing to labor and engineering work on Khufu's pyramid produces a galactic blueprint. We are gaining knowledge of Egyptian pyramid building, but complete knowledge may never exist, except for ancient Egyptian builders. For any number of reasons, modern thinking for some people rejects capabilities of Egyptian builders. In the progression of humanity, Egyptians are modern humans, capable of abstract thinking, forethought, and conceptualizing a future project such as a pyramid.

Current reality has not allowed humanity to duplicate the Great Pyramid or know exactly how it was constructed. We do not have machines that accurately place 80-ton stones such that papers cannot slide between them. To some degree, jealousy permeates our thoughts, since we cannot duplicate Khufu's pyramid, nor do we know how or have capabilities to place 25 to 80-ton stones. Egyptian scholars and historians have labored with the idea that pyramid laborers were slaves. As findings and knowledge increased over the years, a picture of valuable, well fed, and cared for laborers has appeared. To accomplish precision building skills, healthy, strong, and motivated workers are necessary. An idea of 20 years enslavement does not instill laborers with enthusiasm, but life in better living quarters with good, adequate food coupled to medical care would provide life superior to the average Egyptians.

By archaeologists examining fossils, garbage, and remains of the Giza Plateau, a pattern of better food and messing begins to emerge. A ratio of pig bones to cattle bones shows 1:6 and in some areas the ratio was 16:1. Egyptian builders realized a high protein diet was necessary for long, heavy sessions of intense labor. Brain function did not suffer either. When considering the logistics problems of caring for untold thousands of laborers, quarrying granite, limestone, copper, turquoise, and diorite with hammers, an organization conundrum materializes that would seriously challenge any modern construction company. Additive to the conundrum, nearly all mined stones would need an orderly Nile and canal float to be utilized.

With a logistics problem stretching imagination, construction of Khufu's 481 feet tall pyramid was acquired engineering feats beyond modernized equipment's capabilities. Yet, Egyptian architects like Hemiunu and organizers like Merer managed an edifice that weighs 5.75 million tons. For a duration to modern times and beyond, the Great Pyramid is hard to beat.

Did the ancient Egyptians have civilization? If Egyptians are measured by modern criteria, civilization was present in its culture and society. An advanced city is proposed as a criterion. But what does advanced mean when differentiating from modern times to 4,600 years ago? While building the Khufu pyramid, a city fulfilled all the needs of 20,000 workers. Specialized workers were certainly present for technical block placement. Technology was required for building, since weight, direction, fulcrum physics, balance, and future requirements must be understood. Records are normally accepted as a requirement for civility. Tomb and pyramidal hieroglyphs demonstrate long-term record-keeping and are in contention for the longest records. Papyrus records stored at Wadi al-Jarf for better than 4,600 years can also fill criteria for civilization. Social scientists see the capability to produce complex installations as a civilization criterion. Indeed, the Giza Pyramids are complex installations, which modern humans do not understand fully to this day, nor can they be re-created.

Did the ancient Egyptians beat modern humans to civilization and maintain it far longer than any current country or society? If the Egyptian Old Kingdom is considered, 2,686 BC to 2,134 BC, there stands probability of 552 years of civilization. If the beginning years of the Old kingdom are considered, Egyptians beat modern times by over 4,700 years. How do modern time humans interpret archaeological feats that surpass capabilities of modern technology by several thousand years? Many years before modern times, pyramidal edifices were accomplished all over the world.

Chapter 4
CRUSADES

As humanity moved along in history, ideas of control and power became predominant in the mind of Pope Urban II, who called for the First Crusade at the Council of Clermont in 1095. Primarily, Urban desired recovery of the Holy Land, ousting the Muslims, and repression of growing heresy and outright paganism. A desire from Urban and the Catholic Church was insufficient for the monumental task. Urban's word carried power to generate military power from Emperor Alexios I, Emperor of the Byzantine Empire, who welcomed, maybe, 100,000 pilgrims in 1096. These numbers would diminish. Besides the temporary military might, the First Crusade and subsequent crusades badly needed to retain volunteers or pilgrims. If motivational forces were gathered under the Christian causes, Urban might succeed as the head of the Holy Roman Catholic Church for combining Western and Eastern Catholic branches.

Crusade volunteers took vows to receive forbearance and leniency from the church, while others sought total forgiveness, political gain, recognition, and dismissal of debts through previous feudal obligations. What lay before the poorly trained Byzantine army and glory minded volunteers was a conquering of the Holy Land, Nicaea, Dorylaeum, Antioch, and Jerusalem – no small task for a large, well-trained and supplied army.

The first Crusade or the People's Crusade was from 1096 to 1099 and had a primary reason of 3,000 Christian Pilgrims massacred in Jerusalem. Other reasons were to end Turk threat, inspiration from the Council of Clermont, and the "Will of God." The preaching of Peter the Hermit, who occasionally carried a huge cross, was most inspirational for the peasants and poor people. With little or no preparation, supplies, or training these uninformed peasants were eager for a Jerusalem Crusade to correct the Muslim wrong. Led by Peter the Hermit, basically, these "Will of God" peasants crossed the Bosporus and were slaughtered by the Turks. A few survived to follow Peter the Hermit to the walls of Jerusalem.

Via Constantinople and the Bosporus, the more realistic leaders such as Godfrey of Bouillon, Duke of Lorraine, and Tancred captured Nicaea, Antioch, and pushed on to Jerusalem. Their second attempt on the Jerusalem walls was successful, and by July 1099, Jerusalem was in Crusader hands, although a terrible slaughter besieged the infidels. In a few days, only a few Muslims were alive. Time belies the occupancy of Jerusalem, sense it presently contains Jews, Christians of many faiths, and Muslims. The paradox is that Temple Mount is a most religious place for all three religions.

In 1009, a beginning irritant or spark for a crusade to Constantinople may have been caused by the Bishop of Constantinople not listing the Pope or Bishop of Rome on the list of bishops in communion with the Constantinople church. Pope John XVIII, Giovanni Fassano was Pope from 1004 to 1009. Following Pope John XVIII was Pope Sergius IV, born Pietro Martino Buccaporci, who occupied the papacy from 1009 to 1012. The ultimate of insubordinate communication recipient must have felt some loathing from the Constantinople Bishop.

The communiqué carries some weight, since Constantinople was the Byzantine capital and possessed the world's largest Christian occupancy. The Rome – Constantinople disgruntlement continued to 1054; whereby, a papal delegation to Constantinople excommunicated the Bishop. In turn, the Pope of Rome was excommunicated by the Bishop of Constantinople. For part of 1054, Bruno Egisheim-Dagsburg served in the papacy as Pope Leo IX. From the years of animosity and misunderstanding, the reasons for some correction and intervention were growing with the Rome papacy, and by 1204, the fourth Crusade was launched against Constantinople.

The fourth Crusade in 1204 destroyed Constantinople to a degree beyond correctional parameters that included looting and unnecessary destruction. The attack on to the world's largest Christian city that utilized brutality was scandalous to the Orthodox world. Crusader actions were well beyond Christian, orthodoxy, or Catholic mores.

After the marauding, sacking, and looting of Constantinople, the Byzantine Empire's capital, many crusaders selfishly remained to divide the Empire into small states. After capture, the Latin Empire was established with Baldwin of Flanders as Emperor I of Constantinople. Crusader futilities surfaced with time passage when the mini Empire of Nicaea, a splinter state, recaptured Constantinople in 1261. The Empire was reinstated but never to its former size or economic trading power. For added futility, Constantinople was captured by the Ottoman army and Sultan Mehmed II on May 29, 1453. The Ottoman Empire, Turkey, acquired greatness and power with Constantinople eventually becoming a capital again

The rise of Islam in Jerusalem was embarrassing to the papacy, and a crusade populated by people with only high Christian ideals had, at least, a modest chance of victory. In the path of the crusaders would be the Seljugs, Turks connected to the Sunni tradition, who were in Palestine. Their eradication might help in reuniting the Catholic churches of Rome and Constantinople.

In nearly two centuries of Holy Roman Catholic Church attempts to rule the Holy Land and Jerusalem, failure was the end result. The crusaders began in 1096 with the last and, probably, ninth Crusade terminating in 1272. The last Catholic outpost collapsed in 1291. Six crusades were considered major while three garnered mediocre attention. The exact number of crusades, major or minor is unknown.

When initiating the necessity for expansion of the Holy Roman Church Empire, Pope Urban II did not consider the mayhem, devastation, and lawless behaviors the 35,000 to 60,000 soldiers and volunteers would commit on their quest to spread Christianity and Catholicism. A moving group of several thousand untrained or semi trained civilians and militia have a monumental need for a logistics. Generally, crusaders brought few supplies, depending upon people and lands en route to supply their needs. So, while traveling, the crusaders committed crimes and atrocities preceding their deliverance of Christianity and conversions of Muslims to Christians.

In the two century Crusade processes, the lengthy scenario overlooked auspices of civilization and rights of humanity to express disregard for the Pope's and Christian leader's dogma, ideas, and ideals. The lengthy period also exemplifies overriding egos, controlling quests, self-satisfaction, and righteous attitudes of Popes and church leaders in lieu of true Christian and civil teaching.

Chapter 5
Politics in Lieu of Leadership

Has the US allowed politics to replace true leadership? In the last few decades, the quest for presidential, senator, and representative seats has evolved into personal attacks, character assassinations, candidate history investigations for derogatory means, and television debates to defame competing candidates. The nation has allowed the political candidates pursuit to sensationalism and personal degradation. For the most part, sovereignty of the nation remains in the background of discussions. We now emphasize perceived infringements of personal rights, illegal immigration rights, prison rights, sanctuary cities, and a penchant for congressional investigations as a goal of the government. These items may need investigation, but leadership and sovereignty are priorities of the nation.

A proportion of senators and representatives do not understand that leadership cannot be confused with popularity. What do candidates for senator and representative propose and pursue in their candidacy? Popularity is prevalent in the minds of the candidates, yet the real factor is leadership capability, which may not garner popularity but deny election. In essence, candidates and voters must understand the difference between popularity and leadership capabilities. Voters must understand that leadership decisions must be based on what is best for the nation, not for the satisfaction of a certain area of the country. Foresight and a reason can lead to the correct but difficult decision, but it's popularity may not be garnered by those voters who are only concerned with self-indulgence and their "at hand" problems.

To a degree, the US has evolved to a nation where some of the population believe citizenship evokes a right to free items. "Free" is essentially an oxymoron. In some way or manner, items such as education, housing, meals, and medicine, which are passed to needy people, are paid by taxpayers. To those in need, these items may seem free, but for the taxpayer they are not. People in Congress and citizens must realize that citizenship, leadership, and responsibility require realization that sovereignty and country have a price for all. In essence, voters should be cognizant enough to vote for candidates that exude national sovereignty and a free country for all citizens, not a candidate that has gifts for all or has the idea the rich should be taxed an inordinate amount. Currently, the US has politicians and candidates who have ideas contrary to capitalism, which is the same thing as saying they don't like personal freedoms or freedoms for other people.

The adage, "the world is not fair," is still in existence; however, those in congressional leadership positions should strive for fairness in all endeavors. The idea is easier stated than enacted. Certainly, it is incumbent for senators and representatives to dutifully represent their home state, but as national leaders, the need of the nation should be in the forefront of their thinking, not aggrandizement in politics. Reelection jitters is the primary cause for sympathetic constituent thinking, but a two-term limit would help eliminate some localized thinking in lieu of nationalistic thought.

Chapter 6
SELF-INDULGENT CONGRESS

Assuredly, like political members should meet in a caucus to determine the direction of the party and the direction of leadership to be applied. The objectives of a caucus seem unlimited, but some may be too narrow in scope to produce good leadership results. Some congressional members may become enamored in caucuses but must be cognizant of caucus time spent in lieu of leadership needed for their state and country.

From some voters' viewpoints, Congress members wallow in excessive time on reelection campaigns. Congress members may spend a majority of the days' time seeking election funds or supporters and little time on legislative matters for which taxpayers render $174,000 per year. In these endeavors, a Congress member's efforts and actions are misdirected from the reasons voters had elected them, namely, leadership and productive legislation.

The US Congress has produced record tenure for some of its members. Currently, the record shows 56 members of 40 years or more, with John Dingell showing an uninterrupted tenure of over 59 years. Seven members of Congress show more than 50 years of service. The framers of the US Constitution did not have in mind the idea of professional, long serving members, yet Senator Robert C. Byrd served for 51 years. The idea of half-century service for Congress members as the Constitution was written in 1787 was unimaginable, since the average US male lifespan was about 38 years. However, Congress members have far exceeded the old lifespan number with their current seat tenure.

Since 1943, many congressional sessions have argued for term limits, but there are proponents against any limits. One belief is that lawmaking and legislation require professional skills, which come by experience, a requirement for the craft. As freshmen Congress members note, there exists in Congress a maze of procedures, rules, and precedents that exist in the Senate and the

House. Proponents of unlimited tenure proclaim only experience allows members to successfully navigate the labyrinth of regulations, and with limited tenure, members have less time afforded to advance expertise or worthwhile legislation. As a supposition, maybe, the maze of procedures rules and precedents could be streamlined, minimized, or eliminated such that freshmen lawmakers are on an equal footing with senior lawmakers. Is it possible the labyrinth of rules exists to perpetuate longevity in Congress?

Does the lack of term limits eliminate ineffective legislation? Observation of Congress from 2016 to 2019 would indicate a dysfunctional Congress. Effective lawmaking has not been evident. Ardent, serious lawmakers have been rendered ineffective, regardless of a long-lasting tenure. Ineffective congressional leadership rides in a conundrum, and until effective leadership prevails, a dysfunctional Congress will continue. Long tenured, professional legislators seem unable to grasp the will and desire of the people. Meanwhile, civilization receives a penalty due to lack of congressional leadership.

Over 80 percent of the US population see reasons for term limits. The Constitution did not have career or professional politicians in consideration. We cannot have Congress members sit for 30 or 40 years and draw paychecks. Long tenured senators and representatives lose touch with the wants and needs of the people and the America they represent. Originally, Congress members were intended to sit for two terms, if possible, and then move on. But congressional career evolution has occurred, and the idea has not been to the benefit of the nation.

The nation does not need or desire professional politicians. Instead, the country needs new industry professionals who are in touch with the needs of the people and, especially, the country. Fresh politicians have the constitutional right of serving two terms, adding workforce thinking, and applying ideas of modern innovation. Voters need a variety of talents from which to choose. As is known, a long tenured, firmly entrenched political bureaucrat is difficult to defeat. The tenured politician undoubtedly has a political machine that is well established. Long tenure has allowed that. While the original intentions of newly elected Congress members are predominantly aimed at the betterment of the country and their home state, excessive longevity may instill thoughts of aggrandizement, more power, control, reelection, and, possibly, wealth. A maximum of two terms will eliminate these ideas and leave the politician with progressive legislative thoughts.

In our great nation, abounding with leadership and forethought, one wonders how over 1.5 million people were forced to use some kind of transitional housing between late 2008 and late 2009. How did this national faux pas come to be? The Great Recession of 2007 to 2009 increased the number of homeless people. In 2009, about 1.5 million children were homeless, and by 2013, there were nearly 58,000 homeless veterans; nearly 8,000 were female. For the US, approximately 60 percent of the homeless were male. Since there exists no verifiable method of determining the homeless rate or members, all numbers are best estimates. The downside of estimated numbers is that they could be, sadly, much higher.

Reasons for homelessness vary. Where is veteran assistance for wayfaring or homeless veterans? Perhaps affordable housing is no longer affordable, whereby payments are guided by the premise: "charge whatever the market will bear." Inflation, partially due to US indebtedness, may preclude Social Security benefits from funding housing. Natural disasters, mental illness, physical disabilities, drugs, and unemployment are but a few reasons for homeless people. Regardless of the reason, America has a disproportionate, undesirable ratio of homeless compared to the population. Congressional leadership is confronted by many worldly problems, but, somewhere in the mix, home front problems need a fix. Amnesty Information USA indicates there are five times more vacant houses than homeless people.

Hunger in the US is a major problem and can no longer be ignored. The problem is growing in a "rich" country. Of course, if people are homeless, hunger must be close to follow. How much hunger is there? Currently, low income families furnish better than 21 million children to qualify for reduced or free school lunches. That's about 6 percent of the population. This shortage is ancillary to all counties, as all counties in the US have some kind of food shortage. Congressional districts, of course, are included. To help, unemployment is declining in the US due to some manufacturing returning to the country, but immigration is logarithmically increasing to a point where the US is stretched for logistics

Leadership and Congress must incorporate spending efficiency, which is oxymoron to government thinking, and Congress must raise its sights to national problems with the understanding that local problems can certainly evolve to national concerns. Instead of concentrating on monies for reelection, maybe, our senators and representatives could convince corporations to pay a fair wage for a fair day's work to decrease wage inequality. Possibly, CEOs could become cognizant of a "fair" wage for their work. The axiom is: fair is fair.

Chapter 7
SPIRALING NATIONAL DEBT

In world history, no nation but the US has produced a rapidly increasing debt of $22.3 trillion, and the country has people in Congress worried about raising the debt ceiling for continued government operations. Talk of decreasing the national debt is not conversant in Congress, nor to reelection. How did the US get such astronomical debt numbers? Past administrations showed little to no responsibility toward debt reduction, and, currently, Congress has initiated no: curtailment of spending, accountability, or prudent interceding fiscal actions. Efficiency in government spending is an oxymoron.

The baby boomers are not the singular source of the debt problem, but the first of the boomers became 65 in 2011. Boomers started in 1946, just after WWII. They are not at fault, but Social Security, Medicare, and Medicaid must see to their needs. In the next three decades or so, those turning 65 will climb to more than 30 million in numbers, but the working, supporting population will only increase to a little over 20 million. Meanwhile those over 65 are living longer, which requires more assistance for longer periods.

In our ranking of healthcare with other countries, the US gets the least bang for the bucks, or healthcare inefficiency is rampant. The US per capita cost basis is one of the most expensive in the world; yet, the health results are no better than other countries and worse than some countries. Within the US, the cost of some medical procedures is disproportionately high, or some procedures are not required. With large corporations buying or supporting company insurance plans, large hospitals or medical facilities may encourage physicians to embrace certain numbers of patients per day. Not all facilities condone a quota number, but if so, patient time diminishes as does medical care. Along with the large insurance plans covering a multitude of participants, outrageous medical fees may go unnoticed entirely, or the fee is brought to attention long after the fee has been paid.

In the past, Congress decided a prudent move for national cash flow was to borrow monies from foreign entities. Currently, the US owes $6.4 trillion to foreigners, not a number to be taken lightly. In order, the largest debt holders are: China – $1.13 trillion, Japan – $1.02 trillion, Brazil – $313 billion, and Ireland – $287 billion. Unfortunately, these numbers are growing. Numbers on paper are sometimes meaningless, but a few numbers are warranted. US foreign debt is working at 29 percent of our current $22.3 trillion national debt. One wonders how or why Congress allowed foreigners to control so much of our indebtedness? At $6.4 trillion, it is difficult to enforce the ideas of sovereignty or nationalism.

Numbers not often displayed but are nevertheless important: US total interest paid – $3.13 trillion, total US debt: $74 trillion, total US personal debt – $19.7 trillion and student loan debt: $1.6 trillion. Meanwhile, the largest budget items are: Medicare/Medicaid – $1.56 trillion, Social Security – $1.019 trillion, DOD – $636.4 billion, and Federal Pensions – $284.2 billion.

Chapter 8
Moral Decay

The US has become increasingly secular with God taking a lesser position in many public affairs. Some public buildings have been revamped or designed to suit an increasingly godless society. Our forefathers' designs of a nation under God and a quest for freedoms created by morality are being traded through time for behaviors of self-indulgence and hedonism, which are generated by a please all phrase of "political correctness."

Nearly half of the US population believes morality has taken a marked decrease in the last few decades. Reasons vary, but a political desire to accommodate increasing numbers of people from every conceivable background may be a factor. Over the past half century or more, the US has failed to emphasize the concepts under which the nation was formed. Somehow, we have forgotten that America's founders wanted God, morality, freedoms for all, and rules to form civility. While the US is a nation of immigrants, there have been no reasons to change or obliterate our forefathers "concepts of civilization." However, "politically correct" has evolved to a driving force for accommodation. America is accommodating, but constituent citizens should possess morality under God, a sense of freedom, and understand equal rights for all. For new immigrant citizens, a respect for the country in which they are living is necessary.

America was to become a unified nation under carefully crafted guidance from the Constitution and The Bill of Rights. Personal freedoms were guaranteed, which produced the idea of capitalism. Certainly, free citizens used thought, ingenuity, and creativity to fashion machines, agriculture, factories, and civilization for all. These efforts and ideas formed a capitalistic environment from which citizens can prosper and further add to a growing civil society.

But in recent elections, the nation has politicians climbing aboard that see fit to spew anti-capitalistic venom, ludicrous taxation for the rich, free healthcare, free college, and guaranteed wages – even for those not working. In view of classic socialism failures, past and present, socialistic ideas are espoused as the new, saving governmental model which Americans should follow. Worry not, for the socialistic government will supply medical care, parameters for wages, necessary energies, required transportation, and job positions. Under such a regime, incentives in all fields will evaporate. There will exist no incentives for ingenuity, inventiveness, or job excellence. In such a society, the goals for morality decrease and morality decays. In essence, God will disappear and secular humanism will measure morality.

Is the US digressing to the morality of Sodom and Gomorrah and matching the immoral lewdness evolved there? How is it, now, that politicians and states are proposing gruesome abortion laws? Forty-nine percent of Americans see that national morality has fallen. Yet, we have guidance and reason from the past, but in our hedonistic society, goals for gratification and pleasure are not something for adherence.

George Washington observed:

> *Of all the dispositions and habits which lead to political prosperity, religion and morality are indispensable supports. And let us with caution indulge the supposition that morality can be maintained without religion. Whatever may be conceded to the influence of refined education on minds of a peculiar structure, reason and experience both forbid us to expect that national morality can prevail in exclusion of religious principle.*

The idea from yesteryear is clear, but there is a plethora of modern hedonistic, indulgent, introverted reasons to disregard restrictive rules from the archaic past. Certainly, our pleasure seeking could be moderated and supplemented by thoughts or actions toward country, which could serve all indefinitely.

A modern observation from Ronald Reagan could add enlightenment:

> *Without God, there is no virtue because there's no prompting of the conscious. And without God, democracy will not and cannot endure.*

If we ever forget that we are one nation under God, then we will be
a nation gone under.

Examples of America's moral decline are easy observations. A little less than half of American children are born to mothers not married. Marriage, a religious sanctity, is far less a family requirement than a half century ago. While polygamy is still not the norm, it is on the rise in America. Faith leaders' trust by the populace has fallen to just under 40 percent, and church membership is on the decline, while many attend through an obligation. Millennials, our saving population, have little to no biblical outlook, which does not mean they have no faith. For unknown reasons, nearly three-fourths of people who never attend church, have not been invited. For young evangelicals, almost half favor same-sex marriages. Simply stated, if our morals and religious beliefs are on the decline, civilization and sovereignty are in peril for the future.

Secondary education is become an issue for America. In some states, more than desirable, secondary education is teaching much less in history, literature, mathematics, and the sciences. Replacement subjects entails social injustices, sex, and environmentalism. Early education may impart that American history was charged with imperialism, colonialism, exploitation, militarism, and racism.

Several states have become bogged down with gender identity as opposed to birth gender, making way for the bureaucratic legal battles, which have detracted greatly from the objectives of education. The gay, lesbian, and transgender people have been part of humanity for all of history. But the difficulties of assigning same-sex or transgender bathrooms might be delayed for all of secondary education so that schooling efforts are concentrated on learning. So far, 19 states have spent efforts and monies on special bathrooms. Did our forefathers and drafters of the Constitution have these specialized, detractor problems in mind?

In 2015, the US Department of Education released guidelines on the Title IX of the 1972 Education Amendment, which bans discrimination of sex or gender identity. The crux of the rule is that gender identity may be different than birth sex, causing problems with schools, teaching bureaucracy, and moral values.

Chapter 9
COMMON CORE

The common core of education was initiated in 2010 and detailed knowledge through K-12, and since initiation, 41states have been members of the common core standards. For each grade, standards were to be met, and by the end of K-12, students would be ready for work and have the tools for college. From the government viewpoint, the standardization and minimum requirements for each grade seemed the correct ideas. However, it appeared the government was interested in a product, rather than a qualified and capable student – an educated person. Although the Department of Education asked for a budget of $69 billion in 2017, it stated a hands-off on common core.

From earlier days of US education, ideas of right and wrong were quite distinguishable. But modern teaching and thinking, not necessarily better, have generated perceived non-offensive ideas to avoid conflict or offending a particular sect of society. Educational or governing bodies have known that it is impossible to gratify all segments of society. Apparently, this idea has been rendered to obsolescence in a fruitless attempt to please everyone, which comes from the philosophy of "politically correct."

Having a "softer" attitude in our judgmental thinking will conceivably offend fewer and increase popularity. But, while US was growing in its formative years and was subsequently softening right and wrong to ideas of value, the job wasn't getting done. Modernistic ideas of judgment, however, have moved to please everyone, while blatant judgments of right and wrong have "progressed" to individual value ideas. If the fact of the Holocaust is presented in schools, a value judgment may be placed on the happening, rather than a flat "wrong." From the Nazi viewpoint, it was necessary, but from a biblical, ethical, moral, or civilized judgment, the Nazi Holocaust was absolutely wrong. There can be no degrees of value placed upon it. Do we have to relearn that there are right and wrong judgments in the world and that the advancement of civilization requires them? Questions of feelings about dire circumstances are not helping civilization either.

Earlier times secondary schools rewarded genuine accomplishments with first, second, etc., places. Somebody was first and somebody was last – the way of the world. To please everyone, there has grown a reluctance to award degrees of competency. Academics may be getting the same treatment. Political correctness is now more important than declaring someone last in an academic endeavor. Trauma and disappointment are part of living in the world, and for young people not to learn the facts of living does not help morality nor advance civilization as students grow older. Avoidance of the truth in the basics of learning moral values can and will destroy the nation. If the old Roman Empire senators could testify, assurance of this idea would surely be given. We are occupants of the Earth, which is several billion years old and indifferent to us. Regardless of our self-indulgent philosophies, the Earth will continue to have asteroid hits, earthquakes, tectonic plate movements, volcanoes, glaciations, and floods to mention a few atrocities that have and will face humankind. These things are realities that humankind must face, but our soft philosophies of not facing facts or reality are not going to help education progress in the future.

However, in 2016, the Department of Education, DOE, had around 100 subsidies for a budget of over $40 billion. Federal monies are great for education, but the monies also bring federal control and regulation into state and local education boards. Federal mandates through the subsidies removes the intricacies of the state's educational goals. In part, common core aims for students to pass the SAT for college entrance. Scoring high enough for college entrance is a desirable goal, and to ensure students attain the mandated goal, teachers must teach to the test. But the reasoning and logic to reaching ideas in philosophy or the true logic in mathematics, numbers, operations, or the solutions to equations may be avoided. Teachers are certainly tempted to teach the government test for their own longevity. The process may bypass the intricacies of the English language and all the nuances or communication it contains.

The core process tends to remove individualism and promote a homogenization of the education system. Education may be fragmented, thereby, making understanding difficult. For the goal of standard test mastery, valuable teacher education, experience, and philosophical inputs are often overlooked. The local education boards are forced to honor testing and, secondarily, students, a top down organization. Bureaucracy takes precedence over education. The goal of a complete education has been sidetracked.

Chapter 10
NATIONALISM

President Trump has used the term "nationalism" for our country. He did not mean "white nationalism." However, many of the media and leftists quickly jumped on the latter term. Nationalism is not a racist term, nor did President Trump convey racism in the term. Whites do not have a nation, only people in a sovereign union have a nation.

Nationalism cannot be brought into existence by race, language, specific nationalities, labor skills, or political parties. Nationalistic thinking must supersede the singular disciplines and reach for ideas of unity and sovereignty within a large heterogeneous group. If this idea can be accomplished, we have a nation.

A portion of the cohesiveness for nationalism is leadership that provides goals for reaching the realm of sovereign nationalism. America looks for leadership from its three justly created government branches: Executive, Department of Justice, and Congress. The nation has a system of checks and balances, which provide interdependence of the branches. Each branch is equally important, but members of Congress, House, and Senate, have lost sight of their objectives, purposes, and functions. They have become introverted in their thinking with motivations for self, not the nation. When a plurality of senators and representatives become overzealous in self-improvement and self-motivation, nationalism begins to slip. As congressional members began to lose sight of their purpose and function, nationalism begins to receive chips in its unity armor. Personal goals, raising funds, and reelection displace maintenance of sovereignty and unity that bolster nationalism.

Presently, as in the past, several Congress members spend disproportionate time and effort demonstrating their displeasure at the results of the executive branch election. A primary congressional objective: when elections are complete, regardless of results, members should respect leadership and per-form their duties supporting sovereignty and the nation. Whining, complain-ing, and crying for change shows weakness while slowing or stopping necessary legislation. Misguided objectives or none at all from members of Congress greatly detracts from nationalism.

Dissatisfaction with the 2016 presidential election caused many political liberals, particularly those in Congress, to have concern about the validity of the election. Concern was rampant, causing investigative committees to be formed. However, the head investigation was under the judicial department headed by a former FBI head. This judicial committee spent at least $35 mil-lion of taxpayer money, but could find insufficient evidence of collaboration or obstruction of justice. With the investigation, Congress was enamored into allegations and guesswork on findings detrimental to the election for more than two years. Such sidestepping and misguided behaviors of US Congress people should be marked for historians to note the incompetence and lack of legislation for this period.

During the congressional calamity, Congress became dysfunctional, di-vided, and detrimental to the nation. Over a lengthy period that included mul-tiple internal investigations, nationalism took a dive. Congressional in-house concerns and affairs preceded law work and, especially, beneficial legislation. Nationalism might surface later but not as a priority.

What are the components of a sovereign nation? For some, there is a belief that a nation extracts taxes from prosperous companies and people to appor-tion monies to the middle-and lower-class citizens, while assuring the poor or unfortunate receive a minimum stipend. "Free" would be an operable term. When mandates eventually impoverish corporations and the rich, the system will collapse. But for some citizens the hedonistic, socialistic programs is all they can see. Here and now coupled with immediate gratification are the con-stituents of life, while a futuristic outlook for a nation is of no concern. Pre-dominantly, the nation would have two classes of people: the elite and the proletariat. For those who believe in this type of government, they need to study the many countries that embraced socialism and failed. Secretly, for those successful countries that claim socialism, their monies are derived from a cap-italistic, intrapreneurial work ethic.

For sovereignty of a nation, there must be definition to where the nation begins and ends. There must be protected borders or limits to the interior nation. Historical countries had borders that tended to vary. Huns and Cossacks could and would wander across quasi-indefinite borders at will. With variable, unprotected borders, a country has defensive, political, legislative, and true citizen problems. Who owns what?

From America's inception, the country has been and always will be a country of immigrants. Immigration is how the territory became a country and a nation. Early American history is comprised of immigrants. But with the country beginning to show signs of nationalism, immigration was in need of control or vetting of immigrants to ensure they would be assets to the country. Open borders and unchecked immigration are not desirable traits for national growth, protection, and continuance of a great nation where free and intrapreneurial people live.

Nationalism necessitates free citizens governed by universally accepted laws generated under a national Constitution and Bill of Rights. Citizens and the government work within the laws and rights. These laws and rights must prevail, or the nation will be lawless and chaotic. Venezuela presently displays these characteristics. America was produced by a government guaranteeing personal freedoms for intrapreneurship, well-defined protected borders by national defense, and vetted immigrants pursuing citizenship with contributing talents.

The government must support and defend these well-defined concepts. However, there is a contingent in Congress that supports an open border idea. They cannot foresee that a borderless or open border country will invite enemies, criminals, and individuals who are detriments. For those coming to America, the vetting process is a must; still, the process does not mean the country shuns immigrants. Simply put, if the concept of open borders prevails, America as a defined, democratically governed country will slide into oblivion, much as the Roman Empire.

Chapter 11
POLITICALLY CORRECT

The idea of being politically correct in America has been around for decades. For politicians, the term is a weak excuse to escape a prior faux pas or political blunder. During the time frame of the Vietnam conflict, the North Koreans captured the "USS Pueblo" in international waters. By international agreement, international waters begin 12 miles from country shores. North Korea pays no heed to international agreements and claims 50 miles from its shores.

On January 23, 1968, the North Koreans captured the "USS Pueblo" along with 83 sailors. In the process, North Korean gunfire killed two US Navy sailors. North Korean motives are unknown, but attention and diversion to themselves during the US involvement in Vietnam are possibilities.

The 11 months interment for Commander Floyd M. Bucker and his crew resembled nothing like of elements in the UN Prisoner Treatment Covenant. The crew of the "USS Pueblo" was not warring on North Korea, although, technically, the US and North Korea are still at war since 1953. Possibly, the North Koreans were using this incident as a license to even the Korean war score. Who knows?

Meanwhile, the US was in a quandary as what to do. Recommendations varied from a nuclear attack to not aggravating the situation, which might lead to deaths of crewmen. President Johnson took the weak road to "work very hard to keep down any demands for retaliation or any other attacks upon North Korea." President Johnson was worried that misguided or incorrect political rhetoric could direct a killing of the crew in accordance with radical North Korean thinking.

Following the day of the "USS Pueblo" capture, Washington compiled some quite inadequate responses to the North Korean aggression. A protest remark from the United Nations was solicited that did not get a "USS Pueblo" release, nor were the prisoners released. A deployment of US naval forces coupled to reconnaissance proved what was suspected: "USS Pueblo" captured. For deception, tour extensions for military personnel were motions to show US reaction. It proved nothing. Our intelligence was in error. The North Koreans acted upon their own volition, and the best determination was the Russians had no hand in the "USS Pueblo" capture, nor the eleven months interment and interrogations.

Following the embarrassing eleven months of internment, the North Koreans, as directed by Kim Il Sung, decided to allow the release of the crew but not the "USS Pueblo." Such was standard procedure for North Koreans. Release was instigated only after a written apology admitting the "USS Pueblo" had been spying was signed. Further, the US would not spy on North Korea – ever.

Noteworthy, prisoner release was at the pleasure and discretion of North Korea. The US had no influence on the release date. The 11 months interment was proof that US executive powers could not force North Korea powers to a release. "Politically correct" appeared to be at work here. Executive decisions must be based on what is right, not on what is popular or politically correct. Great leaders make decisions that are correct for the nation.

The North Koreans are no dummies. Quite evident was US involvement in Vietnam in 1968, which promised a protracted war. Two battle fronts were not something the US wanted, and, certainly, the North Koreans were quite aware of this fact. US defense could handle a two-front war, but logistics and popularity could be stretched thin. With the North Koreans, the timing for the capture of the "USS Pueblo" was perfect.

Communist collusion is not provable, but the Vietnam Tet Mau Than Offensive began on January 30, 1968, and ended on September 23, 1968. The "USS Pueblo" was captured on January 23, 1968, while the crew was released on December 23, 1968. Did the North Koreans know that Tet would start seven days after the "USS Pueblo" capture? Noteworthy, was the prisoner release exactly three months after Tet. The squabbling of politicians was ineffectual until the US signed the Guild's confession. It appears "politically correct" does not help civilization.

Sadly, the North Koreans used two Mig-21s to shoot down a US Navy EC-121 reconnaissance plane on April 15, 1969, 19 miles from shore. After the attack Mendel Rivers, the National Security Council, and the Joint Chiefs advised and planned reprisals. Any planned attack would have devastated functionality of North Korea. Our North Korean intelligence was weak; so, the US invoked the "politically correct" card and did nothing but resume intelligence flights. Henry Kissinger remarked that the US conduct was weak, indecisive, and unorganized. President Nixon remarked that the North Koreans will never get away with a shoot down again. This remark coupled to a scathing letter of reprimand certainly must have put immeasurable fear in the hearts of the North Korean leaders. Our lack of information, intelligence, and good interservice communication placed the US on the politically correct track again – do nothing.

While fighting the war in Vietnam, the US suffered two devastating blows from a lawless country that imprisons leading or ordinary citizens for breach of protocol. History is replete with North Korean leaders' lies, making future negotiations impossible. For example, the North Koreans lied about not being in international waters for the "USS Pueblo" and the EC-121. Without exception, history has proven the consecutive leaders of North Korea possess internal and external treachery, self-indulgence, and an insatiable quest for power. A politically correct, do nothing, approach for North Korea will historically prove a setback to civilization.

The US lost the "USS Pueblo" during the Johnson presidency and the EC-121 during the Nixon presidency. What is shameful for the country is the "USS Pueblo" remains in possession of North Korea and has been through the Ford, Carter, Reagan, senior Bush, Clinton, G. Bush, Obama, and Trump administrations. Since the Johnson presidency, subsequent administrations have seen fit to ignore the "USS Pueblo" capture problem by a piratical, self-indulgent, and internationally lawless nation, North Korea. History books are ignoring or becoming increasingly bland on facts and learning philosophies from world changing events.

From a retrospect of 50 years and better, history reveals nine US administrations that shamefully ignored the lengthy North Korean possession of a US naval registered ship. The 11-month capture is internationally shameful. The question must be asked: Do world power, sovereign nations allow lawless nations to direct their actions – or, lack of actions? During the times of the "USS Pueblo" and the EC-121 shoot down, why wouldn't the threat of 16-inch guns from a battleship or the bombs from a B-52 aimed at specific areas resolve non-negotiation traits of North Koreans? Underlying negative motives stem from the "politically correct" premise.

Vietnam facets of war are endless, as a number of years in engagement range from the 1950s to 1975. Such a protracted engagement produced many POWs, and for the US, they came from all branches of the military plus some civilians. The Vietnam war tenure was lengthy, but wonderment prevails as to why US POWs weren't released until February 12, 1973. This question falls in line with questions of why the cease bombing of North Vietnam in 1968, and why was Haiphong Harbor not bombed until the Linebacker operation? ROEs, rules of engagement, forbid bombing of Hanoi, the associated oil fields, or Haiphong Harbor before 1972. Complications came from the presence of foreign and US allied ships. During Linebacker II operations, Haiphong Harbor was mined and bombed with an estimated 31 Communist ships in harbor; a probable 12 ships were USSR.

Since1964, the Joint Chiefs recommended a mining of Haiphong Harbor, but President Johnson feared the presence of Russian ships might start WWIII. Additionally, British, French, and other US allied ships were present. Of course, our allies could be warned, but the stigma of "politically correct" was the overriding aggressive deterrent.

Since "politically correct" came into fashion and became a strong factor in international decisions, the advancement of civilization has stalled or, possibly, regressed.

Chapter 12
Common Sense

Learning and experience appear not to be precursors of an ever-decreasing human trait – common sense. Humans are not born with abilities to determine good from bad, evaluate, make comparisons, or grasp relationships. These traits or talents must be learned, usually from teachers or parents who understand the concept of common sense. Learning may come from examples: gravity pulls objects down, boiling water is hot, friendliness is better, cleanliness is better, education helps, and so forth. Intelligence may help us from injury and learning from example: one cannot touch molten iron – common sense.

Common sense might dictate a preference toward responsibility, since responsibility may produce positive results to an activity. Maybe, if we exercise enough common sense, wisdom and the ability to differentiate right from wrong or good from bad might be acquired. From the times of the US Constitution writing, our forefathers exercised degrees of common sense that would form and hold a nation together. Agreement and common sense brought the North and South together over individual freedom and economies of trade. While errors were made in 20th-century wars, common sense was predominant in surrender declarations, which were corrective but observed human rights. However, the dictatorship and totalitarian state of North Korea forbade any common sense usage. Since the close of WWII, US society has become spoiled. To avoid confrontation or quasi-offensive terms like "spoiled," we have evolved progressive left. Easy, better living styles have inculcated the idea.

Philosophically, common sense and politically correct seem remotely related terms, but the latter term is subjective to the former. More than half a century ago nearly all Americans were equipped with the tools from the common sense box. Jaywalking a busy street in New York city during busy hours is not prudent, but jaywalking in a small remote town in Wyoming could be feasible. Common sense works internationally as well. Attacking a friendly and trade cooperative allied country shows a lack of honesty, integrity, respect, responsibility, and ethical attributes, which are derived from common sense. Fair trade talks with a friendly country will produce future beneficial results for at least two countries.

If we gain responsibility and wisdom from common sense, then, these traits infer decency as a positive inter-relational factor. In the distant past when the backbone of the US was predicated on the use of common sense by artisans of it, we realized tangibles don't change, unless modified, but only a person or society changes.

Since the close of WWII, the society in the US has become more self-indulgent. We have invented softer terms for spoiled such as progressive left. Easy, better living styles have inculcated the idea that existence within the US deserves numerous rights, which should automatically be granted by the government, national or local. Those born after the war have become inculcated with the term "human rights." Of course, the nation guarantees human rights, but the term has been construed to mean citizens and immigrants, alike, deserve a plethora of free tangible and intangible assets from the government, which must be furnished and funded by taxpayers.

From what discipline, area, or upbringing is this erroneous idea derived? Selfish, introverted thinking in no way displays nationalistic or sovereign thought. First, we have tenured college and university professors who are teaching the progressive liberal ideas, not knowing or realizing their rights to teach were paid for by soldiers' blood. Secondly, the sweat and energy of workers who labored greatly to build a freedom loving, capitalistic, award giving nation were fundamental to a great America, which grants human rights.

Progressive, liberal thinking politicians, who are heavily entrenched by political machines, are driven by reelection, rather than productive legislation. Popularity is driven by free items on the government: free housing for low income families, free medical care, free college education, a guaranteed minimum wage, and a livable retirement regardless of work record. However, we cannot place all professors and politicians into the left progressive thinking category. There are still people who realize no nation can afford a government giveaway agenda and that sovereignty is in jeopardy, which means that capitalism and freedom are in jeopardy.

The last several decades have encouraged parents to place more responsibility on schools for teaching the necessities of sovereignty and nationalistic thinking. Common sense teaching should be taught and begin at home with the parents – fundamental for beginning school. When many young people reach adulthood, issues of common sense have alluded their habits and thinking. Life for them has evolved to only the here and now with the concern for the pursuit of hedonistic pleasures. How or what do these young, self-centered, adults teach their children? Can or do these young parents explain right from wrong? Do they give a "no" command to their children and explain why? We are working common sense here, which is, without doubt, one of the most important human attributes. The human brain can be utilized to process what is good/bad, right/wrong, or use common sense. Essentially, if parents are devoid of thinking common sense, the children will, most probably, be devoid of common sense as well. Schools, then, receive children who have little to no concept of honesty, responsibility, timeliness, courtesy, or ethical values. Teachers simply do not have the time or resources to impart the traditional skills plus common sense values.

Due to our modern lack of common sense, courts spend needless time deliberating matters that a utilization of common sense could have prevented. The nation has millions of dollars wasted on the deliberation of blame that common sense, if used, could have saved.

Chapter 13
DEPARTMENT OF DEFENSE

For now, and the future, the US has strong defenses. History has proved the necessity of superior offensive forces helps greatly the maintenance of lifestyles and what civilization the US possesses. Generally, the US Department of Defense has maintained the best defense, which comes from excellent offensive capabilities. At the beginnings of WWI and WWII, US defenses were comparatively weak, the nation and the DOD slowly learned the defensive and offensive needs. During WWII, Nazi submarines plundered the US east coast for three years before our defense forces produced the necessary antisubmarine deterrent. Essentially, WWII caught the US flat footed in Pearl Harbor and the East Coast. Warnings and evidence of Japan's determined offensive aspirations toward the US and Honolulu were evident. History is replete with our lack of preparedness for Pearl Harbor, but three years of Nazi torpedoed ships off the US east coast were inexcusable.

When the US did enter WWII against the Nazis, the US was still ill prepared. The German V-2 rocket, ME-262 twin engine jet fighter, along with the Panzer or Panther battle tanks, were formidable and superior weapons. The ME-262 fighter, for example, was not matched in capability until the US produced the F-86 fighter, possibly, the F-80 fighter. How is it that US intelligence had not detected the ideas, manufacturing, and testing of the V-2 rocket or the ME-262. With the twin-engine jet capabilities, the ME-262 had fully a 100 miles per hour advantage over the P-51 US fighter. If the Germans had the capabilities to mass-produce either or both of these weapons, the outcome of WWII might have been different. German tanks had excellent designs, but, fortunately, hasty manufacturing also produced critical field failures.

As America entered the war, regardless of our lack of clandestine intelligence or DOD judgment, Americans and domestic manufacturing quickly picked up the slack and began quality production of necessary war weapons. America's perceived isolationist idea was not going to save the nation. As Hitler climbed the ladder to Chancellor of Germany, bringing along his ideas of Aryan race supremacy devoid of democracy, his eventual defeat was almost an embodiment. Hitler's takeover of Poland on September 1,1939, for his misguided perception of oil acquisition, still, did not deter the US administration's idea of isolationist protection. Germany's acquisition of Poland should have provided a catalytic drive for the Office of Naval Intelligence, ONI, to increased vigilance coupled to defensive, armed intervention. History indicates the US and Great Britain did otherwise. The US stuck with isolationism as a deterrent from the escalating war in Europe, fired by Germans and unbelievable rhetoric espoused by Hitler. For confirmation of WWII, the isolationist idea was blown away by the Axis ally, Japan, with an attack on Pearl Harbor.

What proceeds as sympathy to US isolationism, Prime Minister Neville Chamberlin steadfastly pushed a Great Britain – Germany appeasement program, which culminated in Chamberlin's mind with his "Angelo – German Agreement." Later, the German Foreign Minister, Joachim von Ribbentrop indicated Hitler's scourge at the signing of such an agreement. The signing was on September 30, 1938. Just hours before, Chamberlin, Hitler, Mussolini, and Daladier signed the Munich Agreement, which allowed Germany to annex Sudetenland in Western Czechoslovakia. Hitler was moving quickly, since he had already absorbed Austria.

As observed, neither personnel from the US administration nor ONI were privy or participants to the Munich Agreement signing. Although Chamberlin had committed an inter-nation political faux pas with his acceding to the Munich agreement and his generation of the Anglo – German Agreement, the signing, capitulation, and acceding Sudetenland, Czechoslovakia to Germany was third hand to US intelligence. In less than a year, Germany attacked Poland on September 1, 1939, which began WWII.

Before WWII, German submarines were patrolling US east coast waters. During the German "Happy Times" of January to August 1942, U-boats sank 23 ships in the first month. Admiral Ernest J. King's response was very little. We sent vessels to seek submarines but not to escort the ships badly in need of protection. A passive response on the US coast would have been to do blackouts, but neither the ONI nor Admiral King recommended any such action. Probably, the idea of US isolationism still prevailed, since the Admiralty and the US took very little action against Nazi submarines until April 1942. From British shores to US coastal waters, the German "Happy Times" U-boat saga cost nearly 900 ships. The Atlantic carnage was so bad that US defense leaders did not want the populace to know. To direct attention from U-boat successes and the lack of US preventative actions, the "loose lips sink ships" propaganda program was initiated. However, from the US east coast, one could see the fires and smoke from attacks of U-boats. The indecision and inaction from US military and naval admirals was unbelievable and costly to the nation in matériel and propaganda.

The ONI, apparently, was not influential enough enticing Admiral King to mount armed action against merciless U-boat shipping raids. Such indecision and isolationists perceived safety cost more than 5,000 sailors and passengers upon the high seas. Before US defense thinking and bureaucracy could realize the oceanic mayhem and counter national and international Nazi quests, many people had already died.

The Japanese attack on Pearl Harbor had a prelude of US intelligence, ONI, and Admiralty blunders. Neither the Japanese nor the Germans had humanitarian civilization in mind. Dictatorships and enslavement were the goals, which allowed a few leaders complete power, control, and wealth. Clues for Japanese aggression had been surfacing for years, but when the US cut off the Japanese oil supply, the lowest ranks in the military could figure timely, major reprisals. Although Wake Island was an important, strategic asset to the US, it was not the military haven Pearl Harbor was and is. Again, misinterpretation of intelligence reports and Admiral Husband E. Kimmel's intuition led him to heavily reinforce Wake Island and to a lesser degree Pearl Harbor.

In concert with Admiral Kimmel, Lieutenant General Walter Short believed any attack on Pearl Harbor would come from within planted Japanese sympathetic spies. Therefore, instead of dispersal, aircraft and armored equipment were centralized for control. Since General Short did not believe a Japanese air attack was possible, radar detection was not high on his deterrence list. General Short made the classical mistake where civilization is at risk: never underestimate your enemy, especially when they are technically advanced. On November 27, 1941, Admiral Kimmel and General Short received a war warning from the Pentagon. Both of these high-ranking officers either acted incorrectly or did little. Apparently, Japanese intelligence from the Hawaiian Islands indicated Admiral Kimmel was very predictable, and asset to Japanese attack.

Looking back over decades of history, including WWII, our defense departments contained a few high-ranking individuals that were operating beyond and above their capability levels. In retirement, Admiral Kimmel stated President Roosevelt knew the Japanese would attack Pearl Harbor. Appealing to logic and the secrecy the Japanese were maintaining, it seems impossible that President Roosevelt could "know" of the Pearl Harbor attack. Certainly, clues were evident; for example, the Japanese complete disdain of the oil curtailment.

Overall, the Allied and Axis war was surely another indicator that Earthly civilization has yet to arrive. While we may think civilization is upon us, skirmishes, wars, and national attacks prove the Earth is far from civilized.

Chapter 14
THERMAL NUCLEAR WEAPONS

In our present "civilization," several countries desire to see the need for nuclear weapons for defense purposes. One wonders how humanity is to progress if we perceive eventual eradication of portions of society. We have one Earth on which to live, yet some worldly, human thoughts can justify destroying parts of it. Forever, humanities' reasoning and thoughts will have disparity, but as Earth dwellers, cannot we intellectually break through to meaningful and progressive world coexistence?

History contains justification for using nuclear weapons to eliminate radical, world conquering reasoning from one or two countries and peoples wanting to rule all Earthly beings. Hope follows the historical moments that humanity destroying acts would never need repeating. But the following years produced a multitude of instances whereby some portions of the world's population thought power, control, and world rule should be theirs and belong to no other sovereignty. From their aggrandizement reasoning, several countries are making or retaining thermal nuclear weapons for protection and defense.

Presently, the world has several countries possessing nuclear weapons: United States, China, Russia, France, Pakistan, India, North Korea, United Kingdom, and Israel. To thinking, rational people nuclear powers should reason and communicate through the UN or any means to avoid use of these weapons. The nuclear Weapons Ban Treaty is the first attempt to secure some safety from nuclear weapons use. The treaty was passed in the United Nations on July 7, 2017, and was favored by 122 nations. The instrument is forward-looking and inspires saving humanity. There are approximately 70 signatories, but 50 nations are needed to ratify the treaty, and since the necessary ratification is incomplete, the treaty is not in effect.

The lack of the necessary acceding countries to the treaty gives world humanities insight to radical leadership thinking of some countries. Power and control are still driving forces for signatory abstention to a world peace compelling document. Since the last necessary use of nuclear weapons, three quarters of a century have passed and leaders of humanity cannot acquiesce to a treaty prolonging human existence. Does the lack of world unity on control of world devastating weapons give insight to the state of civilization? We have a long way to go, as there are at least nine nations that possess nuclear capability, and North Korea has seen fit to isolate itself from experienced, peaceful humanitarian ideas.

In the nuclear business, there is hope for civilization. Nuclear power for propulsion came into existence via the Russians in June 1954. The nuclear power plant was to produce electricity. Such an achievement came from discovering U238 contained a small amount of U235, which had slower moving neutrons and more amenable to control. Enrichment of U238 to the desirable U235 was the key process. Nuclear fission chain reaction in a controlling reactor could produce usable energy to the benefit of humankind and advance civilization. Hastiness in the production and use of nuclear reactors, however, brought some catastrophes for humanity and civilization. The Russian Chernobyl accident of April 1986 set nuclear reactor production and use back many years. Rightful fear of fission use struck all of humanity, and, wrongfully discredited its use. The safety test and overlooked procedure produced an uncontrollable nuclear reaction that eventually contaminated approximately 200,000 people as noted by the United Nations. The Chernobyl catastrophe coupled to the Three Mile Island was enough to cast dispersions and doubt on any nuclear reactors. Unfortunately, these catastrophes misled world nuclear reactor and peacefully controlled nuclear fission thinking. Without pro-humanitarian forces and long-range forethought, masses of people saw only the dark side of nuclear power.

With patience, science, and dedication, nuclear reactor power can furnish near endless energy to drive civilization to newer plateaus.

Chapter 15
W W I

A global humanitarian conflict began on July 28, 1914, and lasted until November 11, 1918. The initial reason for WWI were assassinations of Archduke Franz Ferdinand of Austria, heir to the Austria – Hungary throne, and his wife. However, Ferdinand's popularity was diminutive and warranted little mourning. Earlier days of the kingdoms and empires traditionally allowed lineage and inheritance to assume national powers, regardless of actual leadership abilities. The war spontaneously began by Gavrilo Princip's, a Bosnian Serb student, June 28, 1914, assassination of Ferdinand, which caused usurpation of powers and economic concerns as well. July 1914 was replete with diplomatic shuffling, where the belligerents were the United Kingdom, France, and the Russian Empire versus Germany and Austria – Hungary. When Serbia, an ally, continued interference with Bosnia and agreed to only eight of 10 demands by the Central Powers, war was declared by Austria – Hungary, which could last several years.

Initially, the Central Powers had problems communicating. Therefore, Austria – Hungry had assumed support from Germany for the Serbia invasion. Germany was under the impression Austria – Hungary would expand its energy against Russia. France would then be invaded by Germany.

Great Britain had amassed formidable sea power by the early 1900s, and Germany was not ignorant of the fact. Certainly, other countries in the Central Powers were cognizant of Great Britain's naval strength. Additionally, Great Britain possessed an expensive, envious commercial passenger liner fleet. WWI was catalytic to bringing the German submarine to the forefront, but Great Britain's naval power was eventually able to defeat German submarine power.

The sinking of the "RMS Lusitania" on May 7, 1915, by a German submarine may have started US leaders to revamp the pledge to neutrality. Torpedoing the "RMS Lusitania" brought the world and US to realize the senseless loss of 1,198 passengers on the high seas, including 128 Americans. German atrocities on the Atlantic Ocean were numerous, but the British revamped the "HMS Baralong" to be a wolf in sheep wool. U-24 had attacked and sunk White Star liner "Arabic," and while in pursuit, the "Baralong" encountered the "Nicosian," a British steamer, which was under attack by U-27. With trickery, deceit, diversion, and flag switching, Captain Godfrey Herbert sank the U-27. In the minds of the "Baralong" crew members, revenge was in order for the barbaric sinking of the civilian liner "RMS Lusitania." Sailors from the U-27 were not rescued.

When the US joined the Allies on April 6, 1917, the combined force of Great Britain, US, France, and, temporarily, the Russians were overpowering to the Central Powers. Ten million soldiers died, while 70 million soldiers were involved; yet, the Germans continued the pure race concept, condemning true civilization.

Arguments abound on the reasons for WWI. Looking back, the assassination of Ferdinand was only an excuse of self-interested leaders of Austria – Hungry to attack Serbia. An increase in territory, nationalism, and control meant vast imperialism. With the attack, Austria – Hungary's military would be on display for the world to observe, fear, and respect. Reasons for WWI, thus, sprang from leaders' introspective thoughts of control and power, rather than any drive for worldly civilization or, at least, inter-country respect.

Chapter 16
W W I I

Neville Chamberlain's failed negotiations with Hitler, belief of Hitler, and non-aggressive diplomatic attitude highly encouraged Hitler and the Nazis. Chamberlains near laisser-faire approach to the Nazis, gave them a safe incentive for attack of Poland on September 1, 1939. WW II was underway in Europe, and, again, the US played the isolation card. Roosevelt and the Admiralty must have surely guessed that, eventually, the US would be pulled into the war. US east coast shipping was devastated by U-boats until Pearl Harbor shocked the US.

The Axis powers of Germany, Japan, and Italy signed the Tripartite Pact on September 27, 1940, which was a military alliance primarily aimed at the United States. Each signee had expansionist interests that were different from the other Axis countries. In a 1936 treaty by Germany and Italy, Benito Mussolini declared that all European countries will rotate on the Rome – Berlin Axis. Unfortunately, the Axis countries would evolve into aggressive, expansionist powers.

Hitler accused Western powers for the outbreak of WWII due to intervention as Germany invaded Poland, which Hitler previously planned. World domination required vast oil supplies, and Germany severely lacked the necessary oil for world conquering dominance. Germany and Japan had become allies in 1936 with the signing of the Anti-Comintern Pact, essentially an anti-Communist pact.

The 1940s provided several issues for the Axis powers and the future Allies, especially, since the US noticed Japan had taken a serious interest in Chinese markets and natural resources due to expansion motives and Japan's serious lack of energy and other resources. By 1931, Japan's expansionist motives were sufficient for an attack on Manchuria, a rich resource province. The Japanese had the gall to install a government in the province.

The Japanese takeover of Manchuria on September 18, 1931, was well known, but the US continued to play a strong isolationist role guided by Roosevelt and his advisers. Since the Japanese takeover of Manchuria was not recognized by the US, a full-scale war developed in 1937. Until 1941, the US continued supplying energy and steel to Japan for its Chinese conquest – unbelievable. Isolationism was backfiring, but finally, the US froze Japanese assets on July 26, 1941, and stopped oil and gasoline supplies on August 1, 1941.

Japanese atrocities in China were horrific and beyond civilized human mores. Conquering a province was the goal, but burying people alive, torture, and rape are not the characteristics of civilized nations – far from it. The Japanese December 13, 1937, capture of Nanking needlessly cost the lives of nearly 200,000 Chinese soldiers. Unconfirmed deaths could have been as high as 300,000. An uncivilized Japanese act was the burying of live Chinese soldiers. One cannot get farther from civilization than Japan's atrocities. By any civilized thought, these inhuman slaughters indicate true civilization is an unfathomable distance from humankind.

The surrender of Germany at WWI's end presented numerous arrays of Allied demands. After the war, the Treaty of Versailles came into existence by January 10, 1920, to exact punishment and reparations from Germany. Conditions of the treaty are many: pay reparations to Allies, pay the US $31.4 billion, surrender territories seized, accept responsibility for all losses and damages, surrender overseas territories, could possess a small military, could possess no submarines, be stripped of 25,000 square miles, lose seven million people, must cede coal output of Saar coal mines to France for 15 years, must recognize independence of Czechoslovakia, cede parts to Silesia, cede 51,800 square miles to Poland, and cede Danzig to be a free city.

Obedience to the treaty was difficult for a prideful Germany and below its dignity for leaders and much of the populace. In fact, the hate and disdain of the treaty burned badly enough to initiate WWII ambition and aggression. To German leaders and proto-Nazis, the no submarine and small military conditions were detrimental to pride and nationalism. However, contrary to the Treaty of Versailles and before WWII, the Germans wanted to start building U-boats along with crew training, and, with intent, the Germans clandestinely started manufacturing submarines and crew training in the late 1930s. Clearly, the Nazis had no intention of honoring the limited military provision of the treaty, especially naval. Pacts, agreements, or treaties meant nothing to the growing Nazi powers or Hitler. Civilization as a free world attribute was not a plan or foresight of Hitler.

The beginning of World War II saw 65 U-boats with more than 20 at sea. Such a submarine count was proof positive that Germany and Hitler had no intentions of honoring any foregone agreements. Since WWI and during the 1930s, one wonders where the US, Great Britain, and French intelligence operatives were. Although the US was reveling in isolationism, there existed no prohibition on espionage of Germany or Japan. A historical look reveals the building of 65 submarines against the Treaty of Versailles on a shoreline was detectable. As the European WWII started on September 1, 1939, Germany already had over one third of their submarine fleet at sea. No country was prepared, including the US.

Soon after the December 7, 1941, Japanese attack on Pearl Harbor, Germany declared war against the US on December 11, 1941, for "provocations" committed by the US. For this baseless breach of international protocol, the US likewise declared war on Germany later the same day. With the US under attack on two fronts, Hawaii and the Atlantic Ocean, the idea of isolationism, finally, became antiquated and intellectually untenable for American leaders.

For the aggrandizement of Germany, Japan, and Italy, the world's people and the Allies had to pay the price to avoid enslavement and subservience to the Axis powers. The ideas of Axis leaders were quite distant from civilization, free, and self-willed people. The idea of control and power over countries and people are powerful motivators for potential dictators, and, unfortunately, the seeds of power, control, and expansion are planted solidly in the minds of some humans today, which leaves hope for civilization on a precarious balance – still.

Chapter 17
KOREAN WAR

Many wars have been fought in the world's history, but the Korean War's motives compete handily as the weakest known to humanity. North Korea's Kim Il-sung, armed with psychological and material support from China and Russia, crossed the 38th parallel to invade South Korea. The Communist country greedily lusted for more territory and subservient people – or, enslaved people. Socialism was North Korea's motif, underscored by China's and Russia's Communism.

To seize South Korea, North Korea crossed the parallel on June 25, 1950. Syngman Rhee and South Korea were not well equipped militarily. For help, the United Nations Security Council commissioned the United Nations Command to dispatch troops from 21 countries to South Korea. Of course, the US supplied 90 percent of the military personnel. For the first couple of months, the south was near defeat, but in September 1950, an amphibious UN counterattack at Incheon separated many People's Army soldiers to the south. The next month saw UN forces invade North Korea to the Yalu River, a border river. However, October 19 saw Chinese People's Army attacking and crossing the Yalu River, and compelled UN forces to retreat to the 38th parallel by December. Battles cycled back and forth, allowing attrition to become a factor. Areas near the 38th parallel became the battlegrounds.

The Korean War caught the US flat footed. At the outset, President Truman ordered a shipping blockade of North Korea, but the President had not been informed that US warships were not available. The President and Secretary of Defense, Louis Johnson, in their misguided efforts to drastically cut the defense budgets, especially the Navy's, were trapped in their own lair when the Korean War started. Truman was balancing a double edge sword, since he wanted the blockade, but he and Johnson, without judicious forethought, had cut the naval budget so severely that defensive resources were not available. Truman and Johnson had manufactured their own problem. American leaders are slow to learn post war military downgrades are detrimental to the country, even as congressional budget cut zealots dance at their doors.

As history has consistently shown, post war Congresses and presidents want to drastically cut defense budgets because such actions look good and appear fiscally correct. With the Korean War starting, Secretary Johnson quickly approved several billion to the defense budget. From drastic military budget cuts Truman and Johnson accomplished historical back peddling. In Johnson's corrective actions before the House Appropriations Subcommittee, he explained, "In light of the actual fighting that is now in progress, we have reached the point where military considerations clearly outweigh the fiscal considerations." Have we learned? Succeeding history says no.

However, from a national sovereignty viewpoint, a tremendous cutback in defense monies are detrimental to the country. Secretary Johnson (1949-1950) was on the unification trail to drastically cut defense budgets. According to his ideal, and Truman's, the nuclear weapon and strategic bombing concept were the main US deterrents. The Navy and the Marines could be greatly diminished to save costs. Similarly, the Army would need some curtailment as well. As Truman and Johnson saw the defensive picture, the B-36 with atomic weapons was a sufficient deterrent.

Generals and, especially, admirals were in revolt for perceived savings in lieu of a solid defensive posture that included the Navy, Marines, Army, and Air Force. The four-star officers knew from experience that all branches were necessary, including the Marines, which were almost given the boot. History has repeated that long-standing military professionals need to be consulted on fiscal cutback ideas.

After wars, especially WWII, Congress and politicians were swayed into doing popular movements that appeared great for the country, and due to lack of leadership foresight, large or overwhelming defense budget cuts are first and most popular on congressional agendas. The reasoning is: since we won't have any more wars and the world is innately peaceful, defense budget cuts are the politically correct thing to do. Political leaders who rush to the cuts are not stupid, but they do lack long-term foresight and are much too trusting of other countries' leadership abilities. The saying, "Speak softly but carry a big stick," was true before it was iterated or before any civilization had arrived. Until the entire world becomes "civilized," the best defense is a powerful offense. That is not to say the US should appear as if pistols were cocked. Meaningful, thoughtful, intense peaceful negotiations are the first steps to a great world society – civilization.

At the end of WWII, the US Navy had the best fighting fleet in the world, considering our beating at Pearl Harbor. For defense-minded leaders, there are few, pride is in their hearts, but for reelection-minded, money grabbing politicians, the defense budget and existing weapon systems, especially naval ships, were a gold mine for grabbing. Our statesman could be heroes for returning money home, never mind defense of our country. As fighting men returned home, hard assets such as ships and planes were placed on the dockets for mothballing or scrapping. A deficit defense will surely cause a future problem for our country's continued existence.

From the close of WWII by nuclear weapons, our top-drawer defense leaders and thinkers figured the US would have little use for future armies, navies, or marines. Strategic bombing with nuclear weapons would be the sole weapon in future wars. Narrowminded leadership thinking is not confined to any time period and can easily span time, similar to measles and leprosy. From lack of insight, neglect, and ignorance of past experience, congressional politicians predicted all future wars would be fought and won using strategic bombers and nuclear weapons. Poignantly, in only a few months, the Korean War separated these shortsighted generals and politicians from their narrow minded, introverted thinking. The Chinese and Russians would surely take a dim view of nuclear utilization and the fallout during the Korean War.

So, WWII's materials, troops, ships, and armament buildups that were doomed to mothballing and severe congressional budget cuts became the causes of a poor showing at the Korean War beginning. Long before the North Korean attack, US intelligence agencies should have had inklings or clues that Communists were in the land grabbing business. At the Korean War start, US inter-agency communication was not ideal and was further exacerbated by a post war Japan and German problems.

The faux pas hanging on the Korean War was its unfinished state. How is it that US expenditures were $30 billion, 14.1 percent of GDP, in 1953 and equivalent to greater than $340 billion in 2011, yet the best anybody could get was the Korean Armistice Agreement, which did not end the war. To get nowhere, the US lost 36,574 soldiers, had 103,284 wounded soldiers with 7,926 missing, and 4,714 taken as prisoners. To this day, tourism is nonexistent and visitors are not welcome in North Korea. Visitors are likely to become prisoners and subject to torture, as history indicates.

With countries like North Korea on the world's surface with its people enslaved and subject to the whims of a dictator, how distant in time is the world from civilization? Would the geologic time unit be an eon? Probably, since history teaches, but we consistently fail to learn. Have we sentenced ourselves to repetitive mistakes? Yes.

Chapter 18
VIETNAM

The Vietnam War for the US spanned from November 1, 1955, to April 30, 1975; however, difficulties began as Japanese troops occupied Vietnam in September 1940 and remained until August 1945. Japan was warring with China by 1937, and occupation of Vietnam could route materials from China through its southern border for Japanese utilization. Certainly, Vietnam would add to badly needed territories for Japan. The Viet Minh, a Communist front led by Ho Chi Minh, resisted as best they could. When Japan surrendered in 1945, the Viet Minh collected some of the Japanese weapons to begin resistance against the increasing French rule.

Since Ho Chi Minh and the Viet Minh were Communists, and for support, the People's Republic of China, PRC, committed to Vietnamese assistance in mid-1950. The Viet Minh guerrillas began the transition to a real army. But by late 1950, the US was watching the Vietnam transformations and had created the Military Assistance and Advisory Group, to determine the value of French requests, modernization, the training of Vietnamese soldiers, and provision of high-level strategy, if requested. So, the US had a thumb in South East Asia since 1950 or thereabouts. If that year is calculated until 1975, we have 25 years of involvement. Or, if 1956 to 1975 figures are used, there are 19 years involvement. In 1954 the US had invested around $1.0 billion in the French insurgencies in Vietnam, which was lost.

In 1959 South Vietnamese Communist guerrillas started war against the South Vietnamese government, which was a reason for the US to escalate troop levels in the early 1960s. The incident that cemented the US participation in the Vietnam War was the Gulf of Tonkin incident in 1964, whereby shots were fired between a North Vietnamese small, fast attack boat and the "USS Maddox." The battle reports indicated pursuit by three North Vietnamese navy torpedo boats, whereupon, the Maddox fired three warning shots. The torpedo boats returned fire with torpedoes and machine-guns. For defense, the Maddox returned three- and five-inch shells, damaging the three Vietnamese boats. The return fire killed four North Vietnamese sailors and wounded six.

The Gulf of Tonkin incident was not the bloodiest naval battle ever fought, but Congress passed the Gulf of Tonkin Resolution on August 7, 1964, giving President Johnson powers to escalate US military presence in South Vietnam. Before acting, President Johnson was to consult Congress; however, the resolution effectively put the US into full Vietnam involvement.

Since WWII, three battle occurrences presented Generals with what seemed opportunities for nuclear weapons. For Hiroshima and Nagasaki, reasoning and rationale concerning nuclear weapon use will always be under scrutiny, but the overriding consensus involved preservation of freedom and civilization as opposed to Japanese or German slavery and dictatorship.

Beyond those times, wars and skirmishes have befallen civilization, but, so far, world domination has not been achieved. But the Korean War gave General Douglas MacArthur reason and rationale to use nuclear weapons. B-29s were gathered in Guam and subsequently moved to Okinawa. Although

B-29 targets were not authorized north of the 38th parallel, nuclear weapons were threatened if North Korea troops crossed the 38th parallel. While nuclear weapons were threatened by President Truman, the threat of them may have helped in the armistice signing. Finally, no nuclear weapons were used, and the B-29s went home.

At the Battle of Dien Bien Phu, 1954, French and Americans considered a triad use of nuclear weapons. According to Vice President Nixon, a plan drafted by the Joint Chiefs of Staff involved the weapons assisting the French. However, the information on the plan was undocumented and vague, at best.

As the Vietnam War moved to 1968, General William C. Westmoreland had quiet meetings in Okinawa to plan use of nuclear weapons in Vietnam and utilization of them against North Vietnam. The secret nuclear program was called "Fractured Jaw" and would allow use of nukes on short notice. National Security Advisor, Walt W. Rostow, became informed of "Fractured Jaw" and dutifully informed President Lyndon B. Johnson of General Westmoreland's Vietnam nuclear plan. As predicted, President Johnson immediately commanded, "Shut it down." Johnson's reasons were sound: nuclear weapons were not necessary and might escalate to involve China – directly, and Russia's involvement could not be dismissed. In obedience to Johnson, Admiral Sharp sent orders to General Westmoreland to discontinue all planning for "Fractured Jaw."

By 1963, Vietnam generals were colluding a coup for the death of Ngo Dinh Diem, South Vietnam President. Following the coup assassination, South Vietnam encountered political instability, which the Communists appreciated. After the assassination of President Kennedy, Lyndon B. Johnson was handed the Vietnam war, and he followed the domino theory: if Vietnam falls, many other countries will also; success is likewise. 1964 gave Johnson The Gulf of Tonkin Resolution, and with the 1965 attack on the US Army base at Pleiku, which was an airbase as well, Operations Arc Light, Flaming Dart, and Rolling Thunder were initiated for bombardment or ground support. From March 1965 to November 1968, Rolling Thunder used a million tons of missiles, rockets, and bombs on North Vietnam.

Operation Barrel Roll spent efforts and ordinance on the Ho Chi Minh trail, which came through Laos and Cambodia to span into South Vietnam and the Delta. Untold tons of supplies and munitions were transported on the trail from China to numerous Vietnamese destinations. The Ho Chi Minh trail was not a single trail but a network maintained by Viet Cong, Pathet Lao, coolies, and conscripted civilian laborers, but utilization for the trail included soldiers, Viet Cong, North Vietnamese Regular troops, Chinese, bicycles, tanks, artillery, supply trucks of munitions, surface to air missiles, and food. The importance of the Ho Chi Minh trail can be measured by continuous bombing for destruction of goods, munitions, vehicles, and demolition of vulnerable trail positions favorable to landslides, interdiction points, IDPs. Such interdiction might close the trail for days, usually not. From the author's point of view and experience from flying many missions over the Ho Chi Minh trail, work crews or laborers in great numbers would make repairs overnight.

In 1965 President Johnson increased offensive missions on the part of the US and did not assume the South Vietnamese government would defeat Communist guerrillas. Major action would seize this initiative and drive the enemy north. If necessary, extra time would be allowed for final enemy destruction. The US escalation was to defeat the enemy on attrition and degradation of morale. Military estimates for the offensive US actions predicted a victory by 1967 and used the body count idea for gauging measures of success. As time passed, the body count system was tremendously flawed due to erroneous counts, and it could not measure strategic values – success or failures.

The battle of Ia Drang in November 1965 exemplified the US offensive tactic by giving B-52s a tactical role against North Vietnamese regular troops. While US had artillery, Vietnamese regulars stayed close enough to our lines to nullify artillery use. Each side claimed victory, but the US took a good pounding in the Ia Drang battle. As the war proceeded, the NVA, North Vietnamese Army, initiated the larger portion of firefights with a notable amount being well-planned rather than haphazard, casualty heavy attacks.

The year 1967 brought General Nguyen Van Thieu into South Vietnam presidency with Nguyen Cao Ky as his trusted deputy. This rigged election brought some stability to the south. While Thieu's mistakes were extensive, indecision plagued his chances of a solid presidency, yet he remained president until 1975. During this time, US propaganda on successes and victories was increased, since public trust and disillusionment of Vietnam were rapidly growing. President Johnson, concerned over public Vietnam resentment, requested his administration to exercise a minimum of forthrightness or candor when issuing details on military progress in Vietnam. However, as many politicians have noted but have not learned, the public is not as stupid as they may think. Sooner or later of the public learns through any means or external sources information that belies euphemisms dispensed by government leaders. The truth, good, bad, or horrible is far better than lies or falsehoods, which may lead to a labyrinth of fallaciousness to resemble truths. From what media reporting that existed in Vietnam and the administration's reporting through the Pentagon, government credibility became nearly nonexistent.

As the Vietnam War dragged on, morale of Americans and US troops were hitting all-time lows. Much of America wanted a cease-fire, and troops returned home. Dissidents followed by disobedience were becoming factors in military operations. In some instances, dereliction of duty was clear. Unfortunately, marijuana and other drugs became agents to failure of duties. The length of the war was wearing on America and especially US troops and airmen. Many military personnel had multiple tours in South East Asia and Vietnam, including the author. Possibly, an end to the war could be vaguely recognized with the NVA/Viet Cong Easter Offensive of 1972. While the offensive was generally successful, Operation Linebacker halted the aggression.

As politicians knew, Vietnam was central to the 1972 presidential election. George McGovern, Nixon's opponent, wanted a complete and immediate withdrawal of US operations. Also, in 1972, North Vietnam's Le Duc Tho and Henry Kissinger had progressed with secret negotiations. But South Vietnam's Thieu wanted changes to the agreement. To avoid advantages, Hanoi demanded changes, which deadlocked reasonable negotiations. Positive, recognizable actions were required; so, Nixon ordered Linebacker II, which equated to massive bombing of Haiphong Harbor and Hanoi from December 18 to 29, 1972. Success was noted, and all US combat activities ceased on January 15, 1973.

Finally, with a combination of Linebacker Operations and the Kissinger/Tho negotiations, the Paris Peace Accords were signed on January 27, 1973. For the North Vietnamese, the Linebacker Operations and the devastating effects brought agreements, but the North was still to take over the South. Beginning in 1964, long periods of anguish, pain, torture, and imprisonment would end on February 12, 1973, and by the end of March 1973, all American POWs were released. Unfortunately, 1,350 Americans were still missing in action, MIA. What disappoints is that earlier releases could not be affected. In earlier years of the war, politics, especially presidential politics, played heavily on the direction of the war and potential releases of POWs. The North Vietnamese kept the scheduling book. Earlier bombing of Hanoi and Haiphong Harbor might have helped an earlier war termination and POW release.

The year 1975 provided extreme chaos in evacuation for South Vietnamese officials and civilians. Helicopters provided by Operation Frequent Wind was delayed by US Ambassador Graham Marshall's misguided, political idea that an agreement could be made with North Vietnamese taking over Saigon. His idea was costly to South Vietnamese, since many US loyal Vietnamese were left behind, and at the whim of North Vietnamese, they were captured – sad. Marshall's idea of an agreement only delayed the departure of US troops.

What does a look back at the Vietnam War show? First, the end result was that the entire country came under Communist rule, and presently, the country is negotiating peaceful world trade and profitable tourism. The US effort cost the lives of 58,320 servicemen, but the total loss of lives was well over 1.35 million.

Secondly, well over 270,000 US servicemen have some degree of post traumatic syndrome disorder, PTSD, which may not disappear for a lifetime, while permanent physical injuries and disabilities are not easily numbered.

Thirdly, US POWs were finally released after heavy bombing and endless negotiations on Operation Homecoming, which were years overdue. A mighty, powerful, and sovereign nation should not have its servicemen imprisoned as POWs for as much as nine-and-a-half years, such as Floyd James Thompson, or John McCain for five-and-a-half years. After years of imprisonment, 591 POWs were released by the North Vietnamese's' forced hand rather than by their own volition. It is evident, then, the POWs were released only after the Linebacker Operations. Nothing else worked.

Fourth, exactly what did the US and allies receive for a price of nearly $170 billion, maybe more? That price is about $1.0 million a minute. Additive to the price, the "USS Pueblo" and the EC-121 losses must be considered. Although the name Vietnam is still used, officially, the name is Socialist Republic of Vietnam. The Communist Party of Vietnam rules the Socialist Republic, but, unofficially, some capitalistic means provides money for Vietnam. US embargoes against Vietnam were terminated by May 2016. Although in retrospect, they were only marginally effective.

If we carefully consider the results of the Vietnam War by lives lost, prisoner grief, injuries, pain, material losses, family grief, costs, and political ineffectiveness – both sides, how close are we to world civilization? Appearances seem to indicate civilization is a galaxy away due to desires of a determined few to control the masses through socialistic means.

Chapter 19
VENEZUELA

Venezuela or the Bolivarian Republic of Venezuela was colonized by Spain in 1522, but declared independence in 1811. From that time, Venezuela has suffered political turmoil to current times. Occasionally, since 1958 a democratic form of government would surface, but modifications would disguise the republic of democracy. An architect of modified democracy surfaced in Hugo Chavez according to the 1998 election. As president, Chavez was quick to launch the Bolivarian revolution.

By 2000, oil prices began to recover, allowing the tremendous oil reserves of Venezuela to boost the economy. Chavez, apparently, had little regard for future oil price fluctuation and immediately formed populist social welfare policies. For a short time, social spending increased, which was to decrease economic inequality. This program was on a precarious balance due to rapid changes of oil prices, especially if Middle East oil producers, OPEC, decided on an increase of oil production.

Hugo Chavez died in 2013, so a quick handoff election put Nicholas Maduro into the presidency by a disputed narrow margin. Maduro continued the populist policies but with a large gift, a subsidy on fossil fuel, which quickly and largely disrupted the economy. Possibly, it was too much money to the elite and insufficient to the populist proletariat. Under Maduro, the government was guilty of excesses, which precipitated unemployment, economic decline, immeasurable inflation, and poverty, which led to crime, malnutrition, and increased mortality. Under these uncivilized conditions, Venezuelans were migrating by the millions. Most could forecast the rapidly degrading financial situation was not going to improve anytime soon. The same insight indicated government corruption – long lasting. Credit countries were forced to place Venezuela in default: no payment due to low oil prices and citizens were abandoning the country. Inflation numbers for money reached astronomical numbers.

For a look at how Venezuela has fallen from modern civilization, a few examples of how far Hugo Chavez's ideas and socialistic motives would go are warranted. Commandeering, seizure, and nationalization of oil production companies were most favorable to Chavez. Along with Exxon Mobil and Conoco Phillips, OPEC countries' assets were seized for a socialist agenda. The US companies filed arbitration for over $900 million. Larger cases are pending.

Since oil prices were temporarily high in 2008, "farsighted" socialist Chavez elected to place windfall taxes of 50 percent for oil prices over $70/bbl. and 60 percent for oil over $100/bbl. Later, Chavez greedily ceased 11 oil rigs of Helmerick and Payne Inc. along with a large gas injection plant of Williams Cos. Inc. Nationalizations of Venezuela and Chavez continued as plentiful: land grabbing, agriculture, nitrogen fertilizer, farms, banks, glass manufacturing, gold mining, steel production, transportation, and homes for tourism. Neither Venezuela's elite leaders nor Hugo Chavez realized their populist, socialistic goals were not idealistic to other countries, especially pro-capitalistic countries. For high-level socialists, there must be a realization that "free" is really an oxymoron. Seizing foreign companies' assets, money, land, or production under the name of nationalization for country need is piracy and thievery, not glorified acquisitions. In the passage of time, countries that lost assets, US included, will levy long-term embargoes, sanctions, or fines in an attempt to regain assets.

The discovery of oil around Lake Maracaibo in the WWI era pushed Venezuela's economy, but the 2013 Orinoco Basin oil discovery proved to be the largest reserve in the world. Estimates indicate 1.2 trillion barrels of oil with over 500 billion bbl. recoverable, possibly more. With the world's largest oil reserve and indebtedness to the economically powerful nations of the world, some energy thirsty countries like China and Russia might see potentialities in a financially weak, poverty ridden, helpless, population depressed, weak, and leaderless country. Secondly, Communist countries could see great advantage to representation in the western hemisphere with shores only three hours of jet flying time from US southern shores.

With the greed of foreign Communist countries having a zest for control, power, and a thirst for a magnificent oil supply, civilizations driven by democracy under a free, capitalistic people with unfettered elections are many years away for Venezuela.

Chapter 20
DRUGS

The Roman Empire was certainly humanity's early attempt at civilization, and for many years, the Empire ran quite well with many auspices of civilization. Success over time tended to spoil the elite, upper-class and ruling Romans. To enhance the easy life, drugs worked their way into the ruling, upper-class Romans, which soon filtered to all classes of people.

Senators were living the easy life, and soon drugs became part of the easy, opulent lifestyle, which surely impaired some of the Senators judgment. Following handicapped leadership and insight for the Empire, introverted, hedonistic thinking brought corruption from higher to lower levels of the government. Within a few years, lower levels of Roman society were swimming in corruption and immorality in unison with government and its malfunctioning, self-interested manner.

The following examples or scenarios attempt some replicates of Roman behavior that destroyed what was a powerful, noble, and sovereign nation for the ancient times. There is probably no way to portray exact numbers, but statistics indicate the US has well over 20 million people who have some kind of substance abuse problem, followed by nearly five million people fighting substance abuse from prescription drugs. How is it a recent year of opioid overdosing killed considerably more people than soldiers killed in South East Asia. Are we fighting a serious internal war for current clear thinking, whereby, sovereignty should be and was maintained by sober leadership and a sober population?

The US has a heavy national debt problem, which is getting worse as indicated by senators and representatives crying to raise the debt ceiling – their solution. However, citizenry spend over $100 billion on illicit drugs: heroine, methamphetamines, marijuana, cocaine, oxycontin, and derivatives of fentanyl. There are other costly drugs which can become illicit and costly, but the first few have cost US citizens that fee annually. Obviously, these numbers could help our deficit greatly.

The price of illicit drug procurement has cost the nation a fair fraction in relation to our total debt and annual debt. With the additive cost of caring, care cost of affected families, job losses, decreases in manufacturing or individual productivity, healthcare costs for the addictive individuals and those injured, lawyer and incarceration costs, the total prohibitive cost must be earnestly considered. For some time, the nation has been burdened with the price of irresponsible, drug overdosing citizens. Without regard for themselves, others, and the country, these overdosing citizens are costing the US well over $820 billion a year. Only estimates can be made, but the number is probably low.

US consumption of drugs shows and is symptomatic of many drug infested countries: arrests, manufacturing decreases, layoffs, military rejects, dishonorable discharges, overloaded courts, emergency room care for overdose cases, higher insurance premiums, and water contamination including sewage. After a few tests on sewage have been accomplished, the results showed a surprising contamination of: cocaine, methamphetamine, Percocet, oxycodone, hydrocodone, and morphine in sewage samples, especially during and around holidays. It is not known, but if only a few samples were taken and serious contamination was noted, we must be concerned about nationwide water purification processes, especially in tightly budgeted, smaller communities.

For 50 years, the US has been cognizant of a national drug problem, and because of illicit drugs, the nation and communities must divert their attention, energies, money, and efforts toward solving unnecessary drug problems. Legitimate, responsibly handled drugs are not the problem. Illicit, irresponsible, greedy, cash grabbing solicitation coupled to unnecessary, indulgent consumption are the problems. As can be seen, the bigger problem is unnecessary consumption, since illicit manufacturing, sales, and solicitation would be greatly diminished if demand was radically reduced.

From the genesis of drug problems in the US, total costs have been nation turning concerns, but publicizing the facts, costs, and arrests are not favorable to the nation nor the medical profession, which, essentially, has curative intentions. The last 10 years of illicit drugs have cost the US considerably more than $5.0 trillion. Prison populations are nearing one-third capacity with drug criminals. Drug arrests for the last half century are approaching 50 million. Prison incarceration is not a one-time cost. Depending on the sentencing court system, the drug criminal could have a lengthy prison stay on the taxpayer dollar. Rehabilitation, if any, will add to taxpayers' burdens, and rehabilitation for drugs has brought marginal results.

The illicit drugs flowing into the US have many tracks. When drug enforcement people discover one track or network, drug cartels easily switch to another mode or track. If one tunnel is discovered, another quickly opens. Large trucks or ships are good mediums of transportation, because they also transport numbers of legitimate wares or edibles. But the illicit drugs can easily be camouflaged as regular goods, making customs and drug officers jobs difficult.

Within the last few years, manned drug submarines from South America have gained notoriety and have garnered special attention from the US Coast Guard. Drug cartels are well organized; so, intelligence on maritime smuggling, ships or submarines, is difficult to obtain. Originally, the smuggling submarines were quite crude and not capable of great speed or deep diving, but technology has pushed submarine evolution to greater secrecy and speed. Size has increased as well, eliciting more cargo, greater distribution, and more profits. Good submarines are difficult to manufacture clandestinely, which may lead antidrug people to assume there aren't many drug submarines. Such an assumption could be quite erroneous. One rule from the military: never underestimate the enemy. Secondly, do not assume the enemy is stupid or doesn't possess good field reconnaissance or intelligence. Drug submarines have excellent possibilities of transferring their drug cargo. A rendezvous with a ship in international waters at night might provide a workable solution. As the Nazi U-boats did in WWII, a submarine could put its nose ashore in darkness on a favorable, secluded shoreline to transfer illicit drugs. It is not inconceivable that a smart drone could meet a submarine at sea.

The intelligent drone possibility hasn't escaped the drug cartels. They have the manpower and money to match initial smart drone services, because the financial potential of transferring drugs is endless. Since there exists legitimate commercial utilization for sophisticated drones, antidrug officials can safely assume cartels are seeking equal or better sophistication.

Why is it that US is by far the largest prescriber of opioids? A look at a recent year exposed some excesses in prescriptions: over 50 thousand opioid pills per one million people for a single state. That level of opioids demonstrates irresponsibility, placing a significant portion of the population into some state of euphoria. Certainly, this is not a desirable state for people of a sovereign, supreme nation where clear thinking, leadership, and progressive decisions are needed. Not long ago a single state prescribed nearly 800 million opioids in one year. The largest opioid death count appears to be in the middle years of life. Obviously, the dependency on pills and opioids is increasing and detrimental to the country. For nearly 15 years from 1999, opioid prescriptions managed sales four times greater than previous time periods.

Pills, especially, opioids have been fantastic for human pain. However, it is quite clear the medical profession has been over prescribing pain pills and opioids. Like the dependency of domestic animals, large numbers of the population have formed dependency on opioids or other pain pills long after their malady has gone. If regulations remain loose on prescriptions, then physicians and those licensed to prescribe must judiciously prescribe with true pain and evidence, not just patient's perceived need. Logically, prudence must be exercised between medical professions and eagerness coupled to urgency of pharmaceutical companies to sell pills. Pharmaceuticals must realize wellness is the medical goal, not gargantuan pill sales. Modern pills and painkillers are wonderful, if not miracles, but pills are not a substitute for solid medical practices coupled to curative analyses.

How does the nation deal in solving greatly neglected, rampant drug demand problem? The solution will not arrive overnight, but drug education in a few grades before high school and during high school could warn about dependency. A realization that pain pills and opioids are not curative but a temporary means to relieve pain while medical professionals search for a cure, which can persist in life without pain pills. However, there is awareness of diseases or conditions which pain is a full-time detriment.

Certainly, if there exists a large demand for opioids, a cartel, machine, or secretive avenue will come into existence to satisfy the person for a profit, not pain. Since the US has a high demand for opioids, cartels will materialize to satisfy demand and rake in the money, especially if a dependent population can be created.

The US has evolved to a state of excessive demand for opioids and pain pills. Some individuals find the easy access to pills through over prescribing medical professionals and relaxed pharmaceutical regulation a track to euphoria and careless lifestyles. We can run addicts and illicit drug users through courts, criminal systems, and prisons, but the psychological demand and subsequent addictiveness for continued drug use surface as the real problems. The past processes of cycling people through courts, jails, and counseling hasn't provided more than mediocre solutions.

With the nationwide drug problem that visits all facets of American life, where are we in relation to true civilization? Has excessive drug use for a significant proportion of the US population brought degraded thinking, reasoning, and leadership to our country? Certainly, we have citizens who see drug use as a way of life and others who can't face the doldrums or realities of life without drugs. Maybe, civilization can promulgate to the country through a tough realization and determination to arrest the drug excesses.

Chapter 21
US Prisons

How is it that a civilized country like the US has 2.3 million people of its population incarcerated? For the US, that is well over 600 people per 100,000. Modernized countries with at least a functioning secondary school system, the best colleges, and universities in the world should have a minimum number of people incarcerated, not the most in the world. But this situation describes the US penal system. Compared to any other country, the US incarcerates the largest proportion of its population. A large, modern country will undoubtedly have a small percentage of citizens in jail, but providing the education system should allow incentives to professionalism for graduates, whereby, the incarceration rate should remain low. For those in incarceration, the rehabilitation programs should be outstanding.

Unfortunately, the US has a serious prison problem. In 2013, nearly 6.9 million people were in some kind of correctional situation. Has the country found it easier to put people through an agonizingly slow judicial system with possibilities of incarceration than provide sufficient education, or, if guilty, provide a genuine rehabilitation program? For those that qualify, rehabilitation is far cheaper and more rewarding. Depending upon the year calculated, the penal system costs the taxpayer around $80 billion yearly. If eight other countries with incarceration rates per 100,000 are compared, the next closest to the US at 600 plus, is Australia at 160. Japan has the lowest rate at 48.

Not all problems can be solved by gauging statistics, but the incarceration rate for the US is higher by a factor of four as compared to the next highest rate of Australia. For such a disparity, a causal factor or factors must be evident. The tough on crime political rhetoric of the 1970s inhibited rehabilitation programs or restorative actions in deference to incarceration because of re-habilitative expenses.

The war on drugs and political three-strike laws coupled to mandatory sentencing, regardless of the crime, managed to disproportionately load the penal systems, even with people who didn't belong. If ideas like tough on crime and zero-tolerance are added, the US has added a judicial system whereby consideration, reason, and most importantly, judicial thought may have been minimized or, worse, eliminated. Are the record numbers of prisons and those incarcerated systematic of a "by the book" judicial system? Within the judicial system from the early 1990s to early 2000s, life sentences increased over 80 percent for what appears as political motivation.

The US judicial system has some mile markers which are noteworthy compared to other countries. For a record, the US contains the only judicial system that sentences juveniles to life sentences. Of course, in every segment of the population, there exists individuals who have no potential for societal rehabilitation, but within the youth population, potential must exist. It is for a reasoning judicial system to find and not waste individuals of hope. Does our current judiciary and carceral system have the capability and motivation to determine these individuals?

It would seem that aging would decrease the probability of elderly incarceration, since, possibly, we grow wiser. However, our judicial system is showing opposite results, at least by some statistics. In a decade following 1997, 16 southern states have increased elderly prisoner population by 145 percent, and according to The American Civil Liberties Union, elderly, 55 and older, prison population has increased 1,300% since the 1980s. Is this judicial behavior indicative that incarceration is easier than rehabilitation, which costs the taxpayer far less?

Experience has shown there is a difference between mental illnesses and intentional criminality. Certainly, mentally ill people can commit crimes when reasons of mental instability are prevalent. Researchers have indicated there is little or no correlation between a decrease of psychiatric treatment and a disproportionate probability for mentally ill people to be incarcerated. However, in 2005, half of prisoners had experienced some form of mental illness, and jail prisoners were seeing mental illness at 60 percent. For prisoners with no prior record of mental illness, length of incarceration increases probability of mental illness for some, certainly not all.

Policies that have rigid parameters that expedite incarceration, generally, failed to rehabilitate prisoners, and many are worse on release. If incarceration inhibited crime, it would follow the US crime rate would be near the lowest compared to all countries – not the case.

The US has a strong rate of recidivism, returning to prison. In the middle 1990s, one year had a re-arrest rate of nearly 68 percent within three years of release. A study in 2005 of nearly 405,000 prisoners released from 30 state institutions confirmed the rearrests rate, and within five years, nearly 77 percent were rearrested. Of those rearrested and subsequently released again, 57 percent were again arrested.

Clearly, the numbers of prisons and prisoners in the US indicate the judicial/carceral system is not working to the country's benefit. Compared to populations, jails, state prisons, and federal prisons are holding disproportionate numbers. Are we allowing politics in the judicial system along with ease of incarceration to be compared to the hard work of rehabilitation? Surely, when civilization arrives, rehabilitation and contributions by potential prisoners will be of great benefit to the country, rather than a drain on assets.

Chapter 22
ELECTRICAL GRID

By looking at the US electrical grid, evidence of civility and inventiveness are greatly apparent. Although antiquity is becoming a factor in the US system, modernization of grids is underway along with smartening the grids. Before 1992, local power companies didn't always share transmission lines, but the Energy Policy Act of 1992 allowed electric generation companies to access all transmission lines available, regardless of ownership. Regulations, monopolies, and assorted jurisdictional laws prevented general access before 1992, however, the act streamlined transmission abilities and prevented some blackouts.

Ingenuity and inventiveness of US power generating companies have had the foresight to uniformly utilize three-phase, 120 volts, alternating current on synchronous grids. Frequencies are usually the same, but frequency converters can normalize a different frequency. By evolution and design for universality, the US operates on several synchronous grids: Western Interconnection, Eastern Interconnection, Texas Interconnection, Québec Interconnection, and Alaska Interconnection. Each region operates at 60 hertz. The North American Electric Reliability Corporation, NERC, has responsibility of uniformity and that electrical utilities within the region are electrically tied together under normal operations. For greater dependability and safety, the Western and Eastern Interconnections can be tied. Additionally, Western can be tied to Québec and Eastern can be tied to Texas, while Alaska operates independently. From a technical and backup standpoint the system appears foolproof – well, almost.

Unfortunately, an increase in civility brings those who use the associated technology advancement for control, blackmail, or monetary gains. Cartels and criminal organizations can realize power and extortion for control through the latest hacking technologies. For civilization, advances in science and computers are a boon to humankind, but there are those who are parasitic to advancements. Intentionally, those criminally motivated individuals detract on a scale large enough to force industry and protective organizations to spend large sums of money and research to counter, tracking, spamming, invading, controlling, or crashing computers assigned to aid efficiency of, for example, electrical producing companies.

Although the US has regions of electrical power production, they are all interconnected for safety and backup. Can this interconnection be dangerous? To counter grid dangers, the electrical industry is working on a "smart grid." Possibly, cyber safe computers could better manage the grid than micromanaging humans. Of note, cyber safe is not the same as cyber proof, for there probably is no such thing. But continually updated software, programs, and applications for computers can optimize the grid with security, a foremost goal.

As we proceed with civilization's advancement, there lurks serious dangers from cyber-attacks of various country sources. Some sources may be surprising and others may not. Triton, a probable section of the Central Scientific Institute of Chemistry and Mechanics research lab in Moscow, Russia, has cyber-attack interests all over the world. Xenotime, a signature malware of Triton, has already probed at least 20 US electrical system targets. To combat this most secretive intrusion of malware for reconnaissance, redirection, or modification of legitimate computer commands, Fire Eye, a well-established cyber security company, has abilities for malware detection and combat. Also, an industrial control security firm, Dragos, has indicated hackers are running through passwords by using externally accessible ports of networks they care to infiltrate.

For example, Triton has designed malware to disable safety-instrument systems at the Saudi Arabian oil refinery Petro Rabigh in 2017. This cyber-attack was aimed at crippling equipment that monitors for dangerous events that could lead to catastrophes. With Saudi Arabia being one of the biggest oil producers and refiners in the world, Xenotime could quickly develop a world affecting oil shortage situation – control. Dragos has pronounced Xenotime "easily the most dangerous threat activity publicly known."

Xenotime has a proven willingness to interfere with industrial safety producers or programs, and a preference for US electrical grids is evident. Dragos has noted initial operations against the US. In furtherance of US grid spying, the Department of Homeland Security reported a Russian group known as

Palmetto Fusion had gained access to control systems of American power utilities, a morbid call to Russian control and blackouts.

An ability to damage or, even better, control an electrical grid is a world-
shaking event. If multiple grids can be controlled, a nation could be made subservient – unthinkable. It is a must, then, that agencies such as: Federal Energy
Regulatory Commission, North American Electricity Reliability Corporation,
Homeland Security, and the Secretary of Interior place concerted efforts in
protecting the US grid network, which appears vulnerable. Of course, subservient to the grid are thousands of electrically dependent manufacturing and
processing plants.

The sciences of electricity, computers, programs, applications, and software have demonstrated a civility of humankind, but corresponding with the
advancement is a route step of malware. Advances in technology, do not necessarily produce a corresponding advance in humanitarian responses. To get a
free ride, gain control or self-advancement, there nearly always exist those who
would use science and technological progress to their personal benefit or for
a clandestine organization's benefit.

Chapter 23
OCEANIC POLLUTION

As inhabitants of God's world, humans are guilty of polluting the oceans to a punishable degree. For country, industry, or personal reasons, we shamefully and selfishly trashed our oceans so badly that life on Earth, humans included, may be in jeopardy in the next quarter century. The last 200 years have shown humans' phenomenal progress in many areas: manufacturing, medical, transportation, agriculture, communication, and energy production to mention a few. However, we have failed to take care of our precious home, Earth, and its attributes. We have taken advantage of gifts and resources: the atmosphere, ozone, fossil energy, forests, land, fresh water, and vast oceans containing a multitude of sea life. Freely and shamelessly, civilization has consumed but not replenished, protected, guarded, or shown much concern for the environment, especially the oceans, which we are seriously trashing. At our present rate of pollution and non-caring attitude for the Earth, we have but a few years to help Earth and ourselves to survival, not hundreds or thousands. If humanity does not act on our environment responsibly, civilization could be of shorter duration than we ever imagined.

Acting alone, the US cannot clean up or refurbish the oceans of the world. All countries and all peoples of the world must realize we are passengers, or, maybe, parasitic to Earth, and we must seriously clean up and maintain the third planet from the sun, Earth. In the mid-1900s, many people and scientists perceived oceans so expansive with vast abilities for dilution that wastes could be dumped without reservation or future concerns. However, 150 years or less of irresponsible ocean dumping and pollution have shown humanity, the oceans are, indeed, limited on recycling and cleaning abilities. Realization of this fact occurred by a backfire of pollution water, death of ocean life, and human maladies caused by our carelessness. For example, radioactive waste dumping by US companies licensed by the Atomic Energy Commission brought concern to, at least, fishing, canning, food, and shipping industries. If we look at the waste created by humankind in the last few hundred years and compare that to the Earth's age of 4.6 billion years, we can easily see the pollution ratio is unlivable. We are dirtying the planet far faster than it can clean itself, and due to our inattention and ignorance, a few more years of status quo or do nothing will place the Earth in an unlivable state.

A major portion of oceanic pollution comes from the land in some form. Chemicals and particles originate from residential areas, medical or industrial facilities, agricultural runoff, or sewage plants. Types of nutrients, chemicals, or metals entering the ocean are countless; however, chemical combinations occur which deplete or terminate oxygen generation, causing some estuaries to be low enough on oxygen to prevent life. Of course, too much algae can be detrimental, but algae by photosynthesis during daylight hours produces oxygen, but pollutant chemical combinations can block oxygen production.

Pollutants can be cycled by farm animals getting high fish meals containing pollutants. Subsequently, the animals are butchered, marketed, and consumed, returning the pollutants to the consumer – again. Pesticides arriving to marine ecosystems become absorbed into the oceanic food web, which can cause mutations and diseases as they cycle through the human food chain.

For pollutants and contaminants to arrive in the ocean, direct discharge into rivers is a large culprit. While rainwater is a life giver and sustainer, runoff water picks up pesticides, toxins, and poisons, which make their way to the oceans. For further pollution, winds and storms on frontal movements contain some or all previously mentioned elements for eventual oceanic contamination. While states and industries are making efforts to curtail toxic wastes, there are examples of the Raritan and Hudson Rivers on the east coast discharging mercuric wastes, which eventually reaches the Atlantic Ocean.

Still, the largest single pollutants in the oceans is plastic in all imaginable forms. Without doubt, China is the largest plastic pollutants contributor, followed by countries in South East Asia and the Middle East. Of course, the US is certainly a heavy contributor of oceanic plastics. An estimate of oceanic plastic debris would be in the millions of tons – horrific. The initiation of plastic pollutants is unknown, but the late 1940s and the quest for customer convenience might be a Genesis for the invasion of plastics. How did plastics of the world arrive in the ocean? With a large degree of certainty, major rivers of the world are culpable, not because of the natural rivers themselves but because humankind saw the easy, accessible means to discard garbage and unusable items. A truthful statement: we are getting what we deserve – unfortunately.

From the early 1900s, much of the discards of the east coast population were hauled to sea by tugboats and dumped. The ocean dumping procedure seemed a reasonable garbage disposal method, since the Atlantic Ocean is vast, absorbing, and thousands of feet deep. When plastics arrived, about mid-century, plastics for all kinds of medical and hospital use were included in oceanic tugboat dumping. Society was happy because the need for finding and digging expensive land garbage fills disappeared – temporarily. As the refuse piles rolled higher on the ocean floors; tides began picking up the most recent dumps and returning them to eastern shores. In our infinite environmental wisdom, scientists, commissioners, city directors, mayors, and senators did not count on returning garbage – little to no forethought. The ocean and environment did an un-forecasted backfire. While civilization abhors guilt admission of the obvious, we are long past taking advantage of the Earth and its environments.

From the late 1800s, New York City held the record for garbage, and currently produces around 12 to 14 million tons per year, possibly more. Apparently, New York City could not predict a problem with oceanic dumping, but the consequences became apparent in the mid-1930s, whereby the Supreme Court passed a no ocean dumping law. New York is not a singularity in waste production, since over 190 coastal countries still see fit for oceanic dumping, which equates to several million tons per year that the oceans can't handle, now or ever. No one knows, but has humanity with its civilization reached a point of no return? Tons of evidence indicate we are precariously close to an environmental backfire, which the world's advanced societies have caused and may not be able to solve. If humanity will not or cannot solve the environmental problems, then, our horizons are limited.

Would it be correct to say that a civilization would have solved the environmental problems long ago?

As we advance toward civilization, there exists no oceanic part or bottom which is free of humanized pollution. Surely, a remote part such as the Mariana Trench would be garbage free. No, plastic trash bags are found at 36,000 feet of depth. The quantity is few, but the signal is clear: nowhere on Earth is excluded from humans' symptoms of progress – limitless garbage in limitless places.

One of the largest ocean pollutants in the plastics class are cigarette butts. This item strikes us as a belated two-edged sword. Initially, the cigarette smoke pollutes the air we breathe while contaminating the smokers' lungs. When the cigarette completes its atmospheric and lung contamination, the butt is discarded, finds its way to garbage, then, stands a good chance to become an oceanic pollutant. Such a cycle is not singular in comparison to other cyclical processes – chemicals, metals, or bacteria.

Innocence for pollution within the shipping and fishing industries is a rarity. Cargo residues and ballast waters which are discharged can be a real detriment to receiving ports or waterways. Certainly, indigenous marine life in foreign oceans may be discharged with ballast water in a distant port or ocean. For example, native muscles of the Black and Caspian seas were probably transported as part of ballast to the Great Lakes.

Many people are connoisseurs of seafood, and the fishing industry has been eager to satisfy the desires for the marine life appetite. To gain the necessary fish quotas, dollars alone cannot pay the price. Discarded or injured fish provide some pollution, but from the fishing industry, lost or non-recoverable nets are a serious pollution additive. Damaged nets which have lost utility are slovenly left or allowed to sink. Lost each year in the Great Pacific Garbage Patch is between 660,000 and 880,000 tons, possibly more, of lost fishing gear or nets. Other types of discards also mix in the gyre. We will probably never know the yearly total deaths of marine life entangled in floating ghost nets. Recently, many unfortunate whales were caught in abandoned gear and ghost nets. For the present, civilization may not be registering the price of net pollution, but the next few years will make an indelible statement of civilization's disregard.

While the numbers in oceanic pollutants are nearly galactic, civilization's lack of awareness is also without measure. In a recent year the EPA, Environmental Protection Agency, reported the US generated a little less than 260 million tons of waste. Worse yet, two thirds of the garbage were not recycled.

Studies have indicated ecosystems cannot support our present pollution and garbage growth rate, and the collapse can be expected in far less than a century. An estimate of the world's population in 2016 was 7.35 billion people, and in 2015, the population was 7.2 billion people. So, the world had a population increase of approximately 1.5 million people in one year. For 2019, the estimate is 7.7 billion people. From the past, and observation indicates pollutants and refuse increase at nearly a logarithmic rate as the population increases.

Is civilization building its own nemesis? We have but a short time to not only clear the oceans of our self-made pollutants, but we must quickly learn large-scale recycling, reprocessing, and, for sure, reprocessing plastics from civilization to save civilization.

Chapter 24
GREAT LAKES POLLUTION

The Laurentian Great Lakes began forming at the retreat of the last ice age around 14,000 years ago. Probably, Lake Erie filled first about 10,000 years ago, and the other lakes completed filling as recently as 3,000 years ago. To a much lesser degree, water may have been present in the basin over 30,000 years ago with hunting tribes roaming the nearly 300,000 square-mile basin. Some evidence has been found to support human habitation before the ice age glaciers, which started to form in the Pleistocene Epoch about one million years ago. The Pleistocene was roughly 2.58 million to 11.7 thousand years ago and followed the Pliocene Epoch. Paleoanthropology indicates Homo sapiens appeared in the Pleistocene.

As the glaciers receded, waters gradually filled the Great Lakes with pure waters, which remained in that state until humans began cities, populations, industrialization, industrial refuse, and easy "economical" sewage waste dumping. Cities on the circumference of the lakes quickly became symbiotic in their free, easy accessibility to the Great Lakes disposal – initially. Dutifully, history has provided civilization an irrefutable example of gross negligence. From 150 years ago, we began killing our future fresh water supply, which is the largest in the world. It is, indeed, unfortunate that elected major city leadership in many cities is politically oriented and blissfully ignorant of historical and reoccurring environmental damages.

Well over 40 billion gallons of "fresh" water are pulled daily from the Great Lakes. The uses are the usual: irrigation, industrial, public, and livestock maintenance. The culprits for pollution are the normal bulwarks of growth and civilization: agriculture, manufacturing, assorted industries, and sewage. Historically, the Great Lakes have provided surrounding populations with edible and marketable fish, but time and pollutants have brought changes to Great Lakes fishes, whereby mercuric levels are of concern.

While Great Lakes mercury monitoring has been initiated in the last few years, the mercuric levels have been decreasing. However, mercury is a highly toxic metal, which is liquid at room temperature, and it does not break down in time. The freshwater fish in the Great Lakes have a great probability of having mercuric poisoning many times over fish not exposed to mercury. With the consumption of fish exposed to mercury, methylmercury contamination or poisoning, and, unfortunately, childbearing women who have consumed mercury contaminated fish have a very disproportionate chance of bearing a child with unacceptable levels of mercury. Mercuric poisoning has probability for neurological health impairments. Who is to blame for the Mercuric poisoning in the Great Lakes? Essentially, the US is to blame. The population, surrounding cities, and Congress should have had foresight enough to prohibit dumping in the largest freshwater supply in the country, but, instead, ease of dumping, disposal, and money savings were the prevalent factors instead of the country's future existence.

The Great Lakes mercury and other pollutants are significant, since well over 30 million people utilize the lake's water for a multitude of reasons, including drinking. About 84 percent of America's freshwater is the Great Lakes, while over 20 percent of the Earth's freshwater is contained in the Great Lakes.

Currently, the US, surrounding communities, and the Great Lakes Commission are semi-aware of Great Lakes pollution, and concerted efforts are being made to clean up, diminish, or stop pollution. Improvements have been accomplished, but from the point of societal awareness, the lakes were near the point of no return. Throughout the 1900s, especially the last half century, modern civilization's toxins, pesticides, heavy metals, etc., have steadily and increasingly polluted the lakes from almost innumerable sewage and factory plants. The effects on consumers of polluted lake water are long-lasting and accumulative, especially phosphorus in nearly any combination with other chemicals. For future use and consumption, mercury and phosphorus, at the very least, are critical for reduction. Noteworthy, of course, are other numerous harmful pollutants.

As society and culture settled along the Great Lakes shorelines in the 1800s and 1900s, people had foresight or, at least, vague ideas of conservation, but for convenience, ease, and monetary reasons in manufacturing, the Great Lakes became the victims of human discards and dumping. All the lakes were victims of human disregard, but Lake Erie became the easy facility, since the

Detroit River and Cuyahoga River freely dump waste of human activities into it. Locals and observers have declared the lake dead. For introspective reasons, the Great Lakes have existed without substantive oversight or governance, with leaders knowing that 84 percent of US freshwater comes from the Great Lakes. From wrecked vehicles to endless descriptions of refuse lining the shores, Lake Erie has suffered greatly at the hands of humanity's carelessness.

For our and Lake Erie's survival, we must stop polluting it, and we cannot afford to easily call it "dead." With concerted effort over time, the US must rejuvenate the lake from past carelessness and disregards. The current US population, 329 million, surely to increase in coming years, will require many billions of gallons of fresh, drinkable water. Currently, one cannot drink directly from any Lake without direct or latent medical problems. As a nation we cannot lazily, slovenly, or politically let our largest freshwater supply become unusable, for any reason. Although cities have installed efficient sewage plants, we must realize these efforts will not reverse previous damage. We can, however, stop further damage. Correcting previous damages will require a national effort to remove the tons of bottom waste and filter incoming water to realize acceptable levels of toxicity; zero toxicity would be better but probably unrealistic.

Transportation on the Great Lakes has been a boon to America for 150 years, bringing food, livestock, iron, and raw or finished products for use in the US or the world. In the process, considerably more than 20,000 ships are suspected to have sunk, but only three tenths of those suspected are known. Oil tankers, freighters of iron or coal, and ships of manufacturing materials are known to have sunk. These pollutants, **alone,** weigh heavily on the Great Lakes toxicity.

Chapter 25
MEDICAL POLLUTION

Medicine and medical practices have brought humankind from deaths of common diseases of 200 years ago to lifespans many years beyond that expected in the early 1800s. From accidents or diseases of past centuries and decades, the practice of medicine has brought meaning and productive lives to those who would suffer or languish from broken bones or preventable diseases such as smallpox or measles. As civilization progresses, medical practices and medicines have given humanity nothing short of miracles.

But in the physical world, there is always a price for progress and advancement. Medical waste has been with us since the beginning of medical practices. Earlier, possibly, but the late 1980s began to show signs of medical waste on the shores of New York and New Jersey in the weight of tons and innumerable syringes. Dumping unusable equipment, used plastics, in the ocean gave temporary economic feasibility but was far from World Health Organization's recommendations for incineration and care for exhaust gases, which can be toxic.

Proper incineration with care for exhaust fumes presents a safe, viable option for medical wastes. However, if the incineration facility is near the hospital, which is normally in a populated area, escaping fumes and exhausts could release some degree of toxicity to the surrounding population. While the Environmental Protection Agency has issued guidelines on medical waste disposal, there were no minimum standards or mandatory rules for states set. As greater quantities of infectious medical waste were produced, many hospitals found proper waste disposal to be cost prohibitive. Over the years, healthcare costs have risen steadily, making medical waste disposal a financial burden from the waste producing medical facility.

The medical profession has proven itself as a most beneficial asset to humanity, but we must seriously address the contaminated, toxic, infectious, radioactive waste that medical professionals produce on a worldwide basis. Beginning at any facility, doctors, nurses, physician's assistants, staff members and those in charge of waste disposal are at risk. Third World countries may pose greater risks at handling and disposing of waste. In fact, waste may only be relocated since no disposal facility exists. An estimate indicates as much as 25 percent of waste generated by medical facilities is hazardous to and capable of creating environmental and health risks. In poor countries, open burning may be thousands of times higher than any environmental limit, which can be caused by improper ash and dioxin emissions. Of course, if there is open burning, "proper" is of no concern.

As the world's medical facilities and associated waste incineration facilities increase, there surfaces deficiencies in waste management. Where budgets are low, deficiently trained personnel use low cost, incorrect transportation with bogus containers which can be causal to infections. Large hospitals can produce several hundred pounds of medical waste every day, some of which contains body fluids. Sharps such as discarded needles or contaminated surgical instruments may be contained in the waste. Illegal or careless dumping can assuredly put people at risk for all sorts of maladies. The World health Organization, WHO, has estimated 12 percent of HIV cases and 40 percent of hepatitis cases throughout the world are caused by improper medical waste disposal. In certain cases, civilized medical practices are present, but the concerted responsibility to clean up the residues of the advancements are not present. Landfills are the recipients of medical waste in Third World countries, whereby scavengers, dope addicts, and wanton profiteers scavenge for hypodermic needles to sell in the drug market, thereby ensuring the passage of diseases and pathogens. With the numerous possibilities of illicit used needle injections, the chances of inflicting hepatitis B and C are a near certainty. Irresponsible medical disposition of used sharps coupled to illegal and available scavenging robs humanity of health and civilized existence.

What is the cure for medical waste management? Education is a good start for medical waste generated problems. Education is cheap and has a good probability of motivating people in the medical field toward responsible medical waste disposal. Possibly, a broad education could enlighten and deter those in the medical waste scavenge business, illegitimate as it is. Public education can bring to the forefront the hazards of improperly handled medical waste. The EPA advises medical waste incineration is the third largest source of dioxins in atmospheric emissions. For medical waste incineration, those in charge must realize special equipment is necessary which can reach temperatures of 850 to 1,100 degrees Celsius and have the capability of special gas cleaning. If a medical facility does not possess such capabilities, licensed medical waste disposal contractors should be utilized. Most countries mean well for medical services and, probably, waste disposal, but they may not have signed local or international agreements for dispersal. Meanings and intentions are good while actual medical waste disposal is less than regulations require and is without enforcement. To help civilization, the world needs real international cooperation and communication to stop infections and diseases emanating from no or incomplete disposal of medical refuse.

Chapter 26
OZONE

In relation to medical pollution, the gases and other pollutants of medical incineration have a detrimental effect on ozone, O3, that protects all of Earth's inhabitants from deadly, harmful rays. Of course, many other disciplines and facilities are equally guilty of decreasing and inhibiting ozone from protecting and enabling humanity.

Recently, ozone has been blamed for a number of human maladies, mostly lung problems and smog. If we consider the ancient past when life began forming on Earth around 3.5 billion years ago, possibly 4.4 billion years ago, the formation of stromatolites occurred. Layers and layers of cyanobacteria will form stromatolites, but through photosynthesis the cyanobacteria have a byproduct of oxygen. Over the next span of 1.9 to 2.1 billion years, enough oxygen formed at around 2.3 billion years ago to support life. If oxygen is present, ozone can be formed, and some recent findings of sulfur formed 2.2 billion years ago do not show UV light acting upon them-ozone protection. Other fossils show ozone at 2.2 billion years as well.

If ozone was present at 2.2 billion years ago in the stratosphere, then it was catalytic to higher lifeforms than the cyanobacteria. Ozone in the upper stratosphere layers would block most deadly UV rays, allowing plant and animal life to flourish. Simply, if Earth had no ozone in the stratosphere, the surface would be quite barren, and for life to flourish, stratospheric ozone must be present.

The growth of present-day civilization has, unfortunately, given ozone a two-edged sword. Humanity's modernization consisting of factories, sewage, fossil fuel consumption, nitrogen oxide production, and chlorofluocarbons have detrimental effects on the protective qualities of ozone. Fluorine, carbon, and chlorine are the CFCs along with halocarbons have evolved to ozone depleting culprits in the stratosphere. Improper medical waste burning can add CFCs and halocarbons for gas depleting ozone. Recent years have shown significant stratospheric ozone decreases in the vicinity of heavily populated areas, and, correspondingly, these areas show an increase in UVB radiation.

If we look at the world's initial production of oxygen, most probably around 2.3 billion years ago, and propagation of plants and animals since then, the Earth has done well for life. With ample oxygen, ozone became a necessary productive agent for Earth's lifeforms. For life, we must have the sun, but with the sun, some damaging UV radiation arrives with sunlight and warmth as well. Fortunately, ozone has been near Earth since around the formation of oxygen.

A 200-year window on civilization shows an ignorance to the protective powers of stratospheric ozone and a preponderance to produce agents capable of deleting ozone. A comparison of the last 200 years of civilization's depletion of ozone to Earth's production of oxygen and prehistoric level of ozone at some 2.2 billion years ago shows a dangerous decay rate of life protecting ozone.

As cities and civilizations grow, Earth inhabitants complain of smog, largely composed of low-level tropospheric ozone, a large component of photochemical smog. How is it Earth citizens and creators of civilizations producing burned waste byproducts hazardous to ozone complain of tropospheric ozone and smog when we are the cause of it? At times, then, civilization can be and has been its own worst enemy.

Chapter 27
CIVILIZATION AND ASTEROIDS

Earth's history contains plentiful hits by asteroids or comets. Recently, scientists have named the potential of objects colliding with Earth as near-Earth objects or NEOs. In 2013, the city of Chelyabinsk, Russia received a fireball from an asteroid approximately 20 meters wide that exploded some 25 kilometers above the town. The small asteroid injured 1,600 people and caused around $30 million in damages.

A little further back in time, 1908, a probable asteroid of 40 to 60 meters in size exploded over Tunguska, Russia with an estimated power of 5 to 10 megatons of TNT. The overhead explosion leveled more than 2,000 square kilometers of forest. Luckily, the area was basically uninhabited, or millions of casualties could have occurred.

Nearly 50,000 years ago, an area in the southwest US was hit by a meteor from 30 to 50 meters in diameter. The area is now in Arizona and called Meteor Crater or Barringer Crater. For such a small meteor, approximately 175 million tons were removed from a crater .737 of a mile across and 560 feet deep.

To tread deeper in prehistory, the asteroid that hit the Earth 66 million years ago ending the Cretaceous period, Cretaceous-Paleogene extinction event, was six to nine miles wide. This large asteroid, possibly a comet, impacted what is now Chicxulub, Mexico, and buried underneath the Yucatán Peninsula. Since asteroids are generally rich in iridium and the Earth's surface is not, the probability of an asteroid is greater. Scientists Luis and Walter Alvarez have confirmed the high levels of iridium in the Cretaceous-Tertiary, K-T or K-Pg, boundary layer. The Chicxulub asteroid caused mass extinction of 75 percent of plants and animals on Earth. In particular and in favor of humanoids to follow in 65 million years, the non-avian dinosaurs went extinct. In concert, plesiosaurs, mosasaurs, many column sea lifeforms, and much plant life went extinct. Asteroids are completely random, but if a civilization had existed on Earth at the Chicxulub asteroid arrival, it would have been completely eradicated. Lest we forget, 66 million years in the past means little to the solar system or the galaxy. From the time of the Big Bang at around 13.8 billion years ago, the formation of the sun and our solar system at 4.65 billion years ago makes the Earth and Homo sapiens latecomers and junior to the universe. We were absent for over 9 billion years. In our universe relationship, we must realize that we don't know that we don't know. We will be in better shape as a civilization when we know what we don't know.

In the universe's timescale juxtaposition of civilizations and extinction seem irrelevant. By looking at the Great Dying of the Permian-Triassic extinction, findings indicate 96 percent of marine life and 70 percent of terrestrial life disappeared forever. Recovery from the extinction that was marked at the Permian-Triassic boundary took 30 million years with many of life's previous forms missing.

The P-T extinction has been studied as best science can see through 251 million years of Earth's history. For now, a comprehensive extinction appears appropriate, affording change as new evidence surfaces. What event occurred first is unknown, but the Siberian Traps spanned the P-T extinction event with two million years of eruptions and spewing seven million square kilometers of magma. In that broad time span, enormous amounts of methane, CH4, a constituent of natural gas, was spewed into the atmosphere. Such vast, lengthy volcanic action surely changed the Earth's carbon cycle.

Adding to the Permian havoc was the possibility of an asteroid colliding with Earth in what is now Antarctica, and, more specifically, the Wilkes Land 500-kilometer crater is the evidence. However, the cratered date is questionable. But recent gravity measurements reveal its date to about 250 million years ago, which is coincidental to the Permian extinction. This asteroid was four times larger than the asteroid that produced the Cretaceous-Paleogene extinction 184 million years later. Forming a 500-kilometer crater would require a 30-mile diameter asteroid, much larger than the Chicxulub asteroid that killed the dinosaurs. For the Earth, such a collision would produce catastrophe, disaster, death, and weather changes beyond any human imagination. This extinction was close to wiping life on Earth completely out. The human race and civilization are blissfully ignorant of how close we were to not being. We know little of the ultimate changes at the Permian extinction, but the asteroid alone would have assuredly prevented human existence. At the extinction, temperatures would have been 10 to 30 degrees centigrade higher, preventing life, and the 10,000 feet levels in oceans were saturated with carbon dioxide. Nearly all life in the oceans went extinct. Surface sea temperatures were eight degrees centigrade higher than present.

Until recently, an asteroid hit has been discounted, but NASA has indications or fingerprints that a 30-mile diameter asteroid hit the ocean on or near the P-T boundary. Such a hit could exacerbate or cause volcanic eruptions, possibly the Siberian Traps. A 30-mile diameter asteroid hitting the ocean could release enough methane and carbon dioxide into the atmosphere to cause anoxic deaths.

We are getting better at reading the geologic and fossil records, which indicate that in the last 550 million years, Earth has had five major extinctions: Ordovician, Devonian, Permian, Triassic, and Cretaceous. Within these periods, minor extinctions were numerous. Our present civilization has experienced nothing compared to any preceding extinction. We are ignorant of rampant, world changing extinctions, for great extinctions have been the norm in the Earth's geologic history. Unfortunately, the Earth in relation to the Milky Way galaxy or the universe is under constant threat. We must ponder avoidance, survival, or extinction. The probability that Earth will be hit by a significant body is 100 percent. The question is when? Adding to our outlook, Stephen Hawking's book *Brief Answers to the Big Question* remarks that asteroid collision is the biggest threat to the planet.

So far in civilization's meek existence, humanity has shown a preponderance for ingenuity and inventiveness, which may be Earth's saving grace. Many people, including scientists and astronomers, are quite aware of the dangers associated with near Earth objects, NEOs. Congressman George E. Brown initiated a bill that was enacted by Congress to become the George E. Brown, Junior Near-Earth Object Survey Act, whereby NASA was authorized to track, catalog, and characterize near Earth asteroids and comets that were 140 meters or larger. Further, if 90 percent of 140-meter NEOs were located, then, 90 percent of remaining hazards would be eliminated. Potential damage from a 20-meter asteroid is also recognized. Apparently, some of civilization have realized the potential extinction picture, since the George E. Brown, Junior NEO Survey Act has fully tasked NASA with finding, plotting, and mitigating the dangers as necessary. The time span for NASA was 10 years, which has passed, but the efforts continue wholeheartedly despite funding problems. In furtherance, NASA was authorized to commission private enterprise agencies for help in accomplishing this survey act goals. Thankfully, other countries are pursuing similar galactic goals.

To gain a clearer look at hazardous celestial bodies, the total number of asteroids of all sizes that pass within .05 astronomical unit of Earth's orbit is 19,560. In celestial terms, that's within 4.65 million miles of Earth's orbit. There are known NEOs, and what number of unknown celestial bodies is just as dangerous. Of the known NEOs, 897 have an estimated size greater than 1.0 kilometer in diameter, or nearly 3,300 feet. The original premise considered NEOs of diameters 140 meters or larger, a danger to Earth; those greater than 1.0 kilometer could bring catastrophe.

In NEO discourse, the frequency of Earth hits is inversely proportional to size, bigger asteroids hit the Earth far less frequently, but they can cause Cretaceous-Tertiary devastation. The Cretaceous-Paleogene (K-Pg) as the event is now called has the probability of one hit in 100 million years. However, the relative recency of a 66 million-year hit does not mean the Earth has 34 million years of clear sailing. Prediction and prevention require good knowledge of known asteroid and comet population, but a vigilance for unknown celestial bodies must continue or intensify. Since NASA has been charged with NEO detection and mitigation, the agency has created the Planetary Defense Coordination Office, PDCO, to pursue congressionally assigned NEO objectives.

How is NASA and PDCO to proceed with NEO assignments? First, land based sophisticated telescopes can provide nighttime observations. Such telescopes are the Large Synoptic Survey Telescope (LSST), Pan –STARRS, or the Catalina Sky Survey Telescope. But high-quality, earthbound telescopes have limitations due to atmospheric aberrations and airborne impurities. Radar observations provide accurate data for small bodied asteroids that orbit closer to Earth. For NEOs, radar is able to provide more accurate estimates of density. An asteroid's profile of orbit, mass, and velocity are of utmost importance for determination of potential hazards to Earth.

To increase our observational powers and asteroid orbit prediction capabilities, space-based telescopes are needed in geosynchronous orbits or lower. If NASA could place a half meter infrared telescope in the Langranglan (L-1) constant position, synchronous orbit in relation to Earth, tremendous observational advantages could be achieved for asteroids and NEOs. But the cost would be $600 million, an astronomical price. Fortunately, civilization has evolved to a point where we have choices in furthering our lives on Earth and decreasing the probability of a NEO catastrophe. One opinion would call for the L-1 infrared telescope or an equally capable spacecraft. Life and Earth's longevity are worth the price. Another opinion would utilize the best of ground-based telescopes and save money for other NEO detection means. Is there a price to great to save the Earth and humanity?

The realization of dangers posed by near Earth objects have become more prominent in the last 50 years, but thoughts of Earth protection from asteroids or comets emanates from very recent thinking. Science, geology, and paleontology have provided information of Earth's prehistoric catastrophes were caused by asteroids or comets from 66 to 251 million years ago. Celestial dangers are a fact, but the occurrences are so far removed in time, civilization has no cognition of such happenings. However, nonrecognition or blissful ignorance lends nothing to a continuance of survival.

Civilization is late in detection and precautionary measures against earthly collisions from near Earth objects. A few land-based detection systems are in existence or in a construction process. A spaceborne observational platform, perhaps infrared, would be a tremendous additive to Earth systems. A major deterrent to a synchronous infrared detection platform, between the Earth's and the sun's Langranglan (L-1) position, is the cost of $550 to $600 million, a large price to pay. In terms of continued survival, Earth's and civilization's, far greater consequences could be paid by a collision with an unknown asteroid or comet. Ignorance is not bliss.

Chapter 28
IRAN

The Islamic Republic of Iran is based on a revised 1979 Constitution, but the Supreme Leader, Ali Khamenei has had the power to change anything and make final decisions. Directly or indirectly the Supreme Leader controls presidential and parliamentary candidates through the Guardian Council, members of which are appointed or elected by the Supreme Leader. In keeping of government powers in one basket, the Supreme Leader controls military intelligence, security, and powers of war or peace while exercising Commander-in-Chief of military duties.

Essentially, Iran has a dictator couched in Command of Counsel, Parliament, and Commander-in-Chief positions. Since Iran is not democratic, candidates are closer to chosen that elected, children's rights are nil with frequent executions, and women are basically without rights. Leader Khamenei, alone, controls banking, monies, and accounts held in secrecy, which ensure his dictatorial hold on Iran.

The façade for the government goal is world order, global security, justice, and peace, which sounds great, but Iran wants contact with nonaligned countries and elimination of outside influences to the region. As of 2009, Iran had maintained some form of diplomatic relations with 99 members of the United Nations, except the United States and Israel. Interestingly, there exists a controversial relationship between Iran, a Shia Islamic Republic, and Saudi Arabia, a conservative Sunni monarchy. Because of these Islamic religious differences, a truly peaceful relationship between the countries may never exist, a setback for civilization.

The military strength of Iran places the country in the top 15 for global ranking. Iran's forces are comprised of an Army, Air Force, Navy, Revolutionary Guard, and Reserve Force which total a little less than one million troops.

Within the Basij, a civilian reserve of nearly 11 million men and women could be called for service. Although Iran and Iraq have shown past hostilities, they are currently allying, and military activities of Syria, Iraq, and Lebanon have been supported by Iranian monies and military forces. In particular, the Syrian Civil War was supported by thousands of pro-Assad Shiite troops.

Under the Shah of Iran, the military buildup depended on American firms for assembly lines, which produced electronic parts, tanks, guided missiles, and aircraft. The early 1970s saw Iranian firms in the business of finding and repairing foreign acquired weapons. Iranian defense industries became experts at reverse engineering Soviet weapons to include the SAM-7 missile, a Communist Vietnam favorite.

Before the Islamic Revolution, many weapons were purchased and imported from the US. How is it that our intelligence agencies were so short on foresight? Why were US companies selling armament and weapons to Iran? Of course, profits are a great motive for foreign sales. In the early 1970s, the Shaw of Iran wanted to buy 80 F-14 Tomcats and over 700 Phoenix missiles from the US, which President Nixon and Secretary of State Henry Kissinger approved. From the President and Secretary of State, the State Department received the negotiations, whereby the United States Air Force was tasked with delivery and training. In the process, Congress became alarmed at the large quantities of weapons, F-14s and Phoenix missiles, being sold and transported to Iran, then, an ally. Quickly, Congress expanded the 1968 Arms Export Law in 1976 to become The Arms Export Act, which had little to no effect on sales of US manufactured arms sold overseas. Finally, the 1979 Islamic Revolution cast a different shadow on Iran's ally status.

Iran is OPEC's second largest oil exporter before sanctions were placed on its trade. The oil reserves are estimated at nearly 154 billion barrels with natural gas reserves at over 33 trillion cubic meters. In the 1970s, Iran could average several million barrels per day production. As many oil-producing countries realize, fossil energy production for a major part of the national income does not last indefinitely, so Iran wants electrical power through nuclear power.

For a democratically run government, nuclear power plants are an efficient way to furnish electrical power for a growing, prosperous, internationally cooperative nation. By looking at the powers and abilities of Ali Khamenei, Iran is essentially run and operated by a dictator. He is head of all functioning parts of the government with capabilities to replace whomever he chooses. Such powers in a singular person role precludes outside thought to bring Iranian activities within parameters of peaceful international behavior.

From an international and peacekeeping viewpoint, the purpose and degree of uranium 235, U235, enrichment within Iran is of critical international interest. Nuclear power plants require good quantities of uranium ore, basically U238, which can be enriched by a lower grade centrifuge, maybe an IR-1. The enrichment will yield 4 to 5 percent U235, which is satisfactory for a nuclear power plant. When enriching U238 ore furnished by Russia for low enrichment to U235 in reactors, a great deal of the work to 90 percent U235 has been accomplished. Recent history has revealed Iran wants more than 10,000 better grade centrifuges.

The wishes and request of Iran's Ali Khamenei for more upgraded centrifuges lends greatly to Iran's desires to be a nuclear power. But Iran has acceded, as current information indicates, to the International Atomic Energy Agency parameters for enrichment, 3.67 percent on U235, not more than 300 kilograms of enriched U235, and slightly over 6,100 centrifuges. The IAEA and EU would like monitoring and no notice inspections.

If nuclear criteria are met, then, peaceful coexistence can propagate for the world and civilization. However, the history and current aggressive action of Iran on the Strait of Hormuz between the Persian Gulf and the Gulf of Oman, a strategic chokepoint for shipping – especially oil tanker movement – leaves the world wondering about Iran's and Khamenei's civil intentions. Still, peaceful civilization remains in a precarious balance for humanity.

Of late, Iran continues to operate outside of humanitarian mores by expanding the ideas of Islamic revolution upon Syria, Yemen, Israel, and rocket attacks against Saudi Arabia. The large oil refinery attack in Saudi Arabia combined with oil tanker hijacking indicates Ali Khamenei and Iran have intentions to affect or control world oil trafficking. Together, Khamenei and President Hassan Rouhani must realize the world will not indefinitely tolerate attacks against civilization in the name of sacred revolution and a nation that cannot exist and cooperate from within its borders.

The Iranian tanker hijacking and major refinery attack on a sovereign country are truly deserving of countermeasures that incorporate punishment. But civilized countries and the UN are acting with restraint in hopes Ali Khamenei and Hassan Rouhani will realize a war is futile and that the entire world does not share their revolutionary ideals. From history's experience and general moral thinking of most civil countries, leaders would consider repatriation after war a finish to world conquering and controlling ideas. Repatriation is proportional to damages inflicted, time consumed, expenses, and benevolent efforts. Always, there remains doubt if anti-humanitarian, hostile to civility aggressive leader thinking has changed or, merely, gone subconscious. Hopefully, the majority of cultures obedient to morality and mores of civility will prevail.

Chapter 29
North Korea

Within the history of humanity and civilization, North Korea is a standout against human rights and personal freedoms. The Democratic People's Republic of Korea, DPRK, has been called a monarchy, or through Kim Il-sung, Kim Jong-il, and Kim Jong-un, the country has become a hereditary dictatorship. Regardless of bureaucratic offices and those officious looking, select puppets handling reams of paperwork, elusive freedom is granted only by a dictator and, possibly, a very limited insider cadre.

North Korea's Constitution belies three branches of government. The Cabinet of North Korea vests the Executive power and is currently headed by Premier Pak Pong-ju. The premier's authority extends over chairman, vice premiers, ministers, chief secretary, Central Bank president, and many other government functioning offices. But the premier's power is far subordinated to Kim Jong-un and his dictatorial powers.

Legislature is under the unicamerally operated Supreme People's Assembly. The assembly has nearly 690 members, who occupy their seats for five years. Carefully selected deputies elect those who will operate the SPA. While the Assembly can present domestic or international policies, appoint members, or review state economic plans, it is interesting to note the Assembly cannot pass or accomplish anything outside party auspices. Kim Jong-un oversees all activities. The State Affairs Commission of North Korea gives guidance on affairs affecting North Korean sovereignty. The Commission's prime concern is defense, which places the Ministry of Peoples Armed Forces under the commission's guidance.

History has seen the Korean Peninsula passed around as a stepchild. After the Russo-Japanese War, Japan occupied Korea from 1910 until 1945 and the capitulation of Japan at the end of WWII. Russian Communism could not overcome greed for another satellite country, so Soviet General Terentii Shtykov established the Soviet Civil Authority for North Korea in late 1945, since World War II divided the Korean Peninsula into North and South at the 38th parallel. Temporarily, the South was occupied by representatives of the United States and allies.

In North Korea, General Shtykov was quick to establish Soviet rule by inculcating North Koreans with communism and the auspices of socialism by nationalizing industries. To ensure correct communistic thinking, Shtykov sent delegations to Moscow and Seoul for consideration of the North Korean future. Through Shtykov, the Soviet Union supported Kim il-sung, the new chairman to oversee the Provisional People's Committee for North Korea. For further Communist entrenchment, Shtykov made a land reform that ended North Korea's stratified class system, which caused powerful landlords and remaining Japanese collaborators to flee south. By 1948, the Democratic People's Republic of Korea, DPRK, was fully communistic with General Shtykov as the Soviet Ambassador and Kim Il-sung beginning a lineage of Communist, dictatorial premier leadership.

South Korean citizens were growing tired of the provisional Allied Military Government and for reasons of self-government rose up against the militaristic governance. The plea for a South Korean government was understandable, and the government was not to be communistic. On May 1, 1948, the South declared statehood with Syngman Rhee as the fervent anti-communist leader.

For the Communists of North Korea and encouragement of China and Russia, greed for South Korea, it's industry, and people caused an invasion on June 25, 1950. Fortunately, UN forces led by the US, returned Communist troops to near the Chinese border. The back and forth pushes finally ended on July 27, 1953, with a nebulous armistice which restored the 38th parallel. Strong anti-communists contingents remained in South Korea, while the DPRK saw any US forces as imperialist occupations. With the existent Korean Peninsula situation and a propensity of worsening international conditions under leadership of Kim Jong-il, true world civilization has some distance to go.

While a strong penchant for world Communist domination exists, North Korea has a desire to be a nuclear power, maybe, due to a lineage of Kim isolationist theories. By October 9, 2006, North Korea and Kim Jong-Il wanted the world to know North Korea had a nuclear weapon. After Kim Jong-il died on December 17, 2011, Kim Jong-un threatened test missiles with Guam range, 2200 miles. Kim Jong-un continues to fire missiles, and his pursuit of hydrogen weapons is essentially unknown. When the Soviet bloc collapsed in November of 1989 and into the 1990s, North Korea's Communist foreign policies went amiss, for the Soviet Union was the bulwark of Communism. Still, China remained the closest ally of North Korea.

The track record of North Korea for international peace is far from sterling clean. The 1983 Rangoon and 1987 South Korea airliner bombings placed North Korea on the terrorist sponsor list. Subsequently, North Korea was removed, and, again was placed on the terrorist sponsor list. Earlier, Kim il-sung had proposed a federation between the Koreas, but general opinion of trust has prevented any federation. Nine countries, including the US, do not recognize the DPRK, while socialist countries such as Laos, Cambodia, and Vietnam do.

Under the Communist regime of North Korea, the lack of human rights is a big issue with most nations. Amnesty International reports of severe restrictions on freedoms of movements, political or personal expressions, or associations with nonapproved peoples. Such activities outside of party parameters could easily lead to executions, detention, torture, or treatment contrary to human mores. The North Korean State Security Department stands as the bastion for behavioral adjustment, except that corrective actions are not allowed, as punishment is dispensed immediately. Contrary to humanitarian mores, State Security sees the necessity of generational punishment in that the whole family may go to a labor camp. Due process or a legal trial is not part of the security process. Unless the "perpetrator" has a friend in a high government position, release is not a hope.

A Human Rights Council established in 2013, known as the Commission, speaks of North Korean humanitarian violations that have no counterpart in the current world. In some cases, North Korea is not as isolated that its own propaganda prophesizes. International abductions are carried out by North Korea, probably under the guidance of the State Security Department. Originality must be handed to the North Koreans for abducting people on an international scale, which is draconian and intense in number. Apparently, North Korea has gotten away with abduction since 1950. When discovered, apparently not often, homeland countries of abductees should object through the UN or any other means to point out North Korea's international violence against humanity.

Through testimonials about North Korea, total control zones encompass humans in forced labor, medical experimentation, forced abortions, starvation, murder, torture, rape, and persecution for any imaginable reason. Disappearances of persons conveying any contrary party thought is common. Death or labor camp are probable outcomes. Unfortunately, there are estimates of 10,000 prisoners or more dying in North Korean prisons. Women in North Korea do not fare very well, since they are subjugated to sexual violence, undressed sexual contact, or rape with abortion possibilities. For women, rules of protection do not exist, and if existent, they are not enforced. A paradox exists since the people abusing women are the ones in enforcement. North Korean women know little of humanitarian mores and expect abuse as a part of life. Of course, the DPRK rejects atrocities against women and calls such accusations propaganda or smearing bad press.

To enforce law, judges are actually appointed by the Worker's Party of Korea, proponents of socialism and government righteousness. State propaganda demands absolute obedience to the Supreme Leader, Kim Jong-un, and to ensure absolute public or private obedience, state surveillance permeates private and public activity. Contrary expressions are noted by strategically placed apparatus, and if warranted, public executions terrorize the populace into desired DPRK obedience. By methods that are barbaric at best, the populace is terrorized to subservience and absolute obedience. Under such a system, imagination, inventiveness, and progressive thought are without origination. Apparently, the public/private surveillance system works well for the DPRK, since 100,000, plus or minus 20,000, political prisoners are in four political camps. Being repatriated is a rarity, but death as escape is common.

Discrimination based on Songbun is a North Korean tool placing people and families in positions and locations as best perceived by the government. While Songbun is powerful and extensive, it freely uses criteria as family history, historical loyalty to the government, school performance, and relationships. The government uses it for best suited marriages, types of work, villages for living, and studies for those suitable for levels of education. If Songbun places an individual high enough in status, Pyongyang may be available, and if a lower status is governmentally perceived, a mountain village may be an individual's choice – for life. Outside of societal mores, Songbun prioritizes ample food to those at higher levels of Songbun, while those in lower levels may be operating near starvation. In fact, confiscation and re-disposition of food to the elite reaches back to prehistoric times for food distribution.

For rogue nations, North Korea and Iran exhibit the parameters of societal and cultural nonconformity in the treatment of populations. From 1980, North Korea had sold domestically produced weapons to Iran, and there exists cooperation and exchanges of education, science, and cultural ideas. Although not confirmed, exchanges of nuclear weapon technology or hardware may have occurred. In any case, North Korea has sold missiles to Iran.

For nearly three quarters of a century, North Korea or DPRK has been problematic to world cultures, and the lineage leading to Kim Jong-un reinforces a continuance of discrimination and hereditary dictatorship, which concentrates heavily on upper-level self-indulgence. Continuance of North Korea's existence depends upon oppression, enslavement, propaganda, threats of incarceration, incarceration, Songbun discrimination, socialism, communism, and a closed system for any education, to name a few subordinating tools.

Ingenuity, inventiveness, and scientific advances are accelerated in countries touting personal freedoms working within a capitalistic society. Countries such as North Korea or the Democratic People's Republic of Korea will struggle forever in the world's society, for subjugation and enslavement will forever curtail and inhibit intrapreneurial inventiveness. North Korea is not part of civilization, nor does it resemble it. Civilization must be underwritten by free citizens in pursuit of goals supported by a free capitalistic Republic, such as America.

Chapter 30
FOOD WASTE

The civilized world has in the last few years increased food waste to 1.3 billion tons, an unbelievable amount. Somehow, the world has increased to 815 million hungry people, which the wasted food could feed several times over. US dollar cost annually is over $2.5 trillion. Such a loss is incomprehensible, yet politicians continue without notice. Saving even a small percentage of this amount of wasted money would be a miracle for a politician, but the real issue is millions of hungry or starving people. Civilization lacks some character when adults and children acquire a serious death threatening malady or disease that can easily be avoided by sufficient nourishment – ample food, curtailment of waste.

There is differentiation between food loss and waste. Loss occurs somewhere between seed and produce transportation, while waste is the scrapping or disposal of foods that are fit for human consumption. Loss is more prevalent in third world or low-income countries and may be attributed to processing, storage, or transportation. A low- income country may lose well over 75 percent in production with a very low percentage of food wasted by consumers. Because of better equipment, storage, refrigeration, and transportation, the US, Canada, New Zealand, Australia, Micronesia, Polynesia, and other higher income countries lose slightly over 30 percent in production, but considerably more than half is wasted by consumers.

Countries with generally low income per family have a food consumption rate of 450 to 460 kilograms per capita each year, while countries of higher income have a consumption rate of nearly double that of lower income countries. To the dismay of efficient production, abundance may be causal to waste. In the US, shoppers want a plethora of items on shelves. Variety is a contingency for consumers while price may be secondary, but with the plentiful stocking theory, many articles will pass the "sell by" date, which means a discard for the grocery. In many cases, items past the "sell by" are still good. The USDA, United States Department of Agriculture, may assign grades to perishables based on criteria such as size, texture, shape, or color, and grocers, while not required, normally follow the grading criteria. So, perishables that do not meet the criteria in some fashion are not shelved but discarded, even though the nourishment is equal to shelved items – waste.

Labeling of fruits and vegetables can lead to consumer food waste, since "best buy" and "sell by" are labels set by producers or manufacturers. These labels do not mean no consumption after the dates. The product or perishables should be consumed before the "use by." However, the "best by" and "sell by" nomenclature causes consumers to clear refrigerators after the dates – waste. In European markets, nearly 90 million tons of food are wasted due to date labeling.

When food is wasted or lost, many resources are wasted in consort. For example, land for crops, fuel for marketing, water, and labor are wasted as well as food loss. Most people enjoy rice, but it takes 4,000 to 5,000 liters of water per kilogram of rice produced. One and a half feet of water in a rice field appears ideal for the four- to five-month maturity. For a prediction, an acre of growth will produce about four tons of rice.

Various crops, especially rice, need a disproportionate amount of fresh water before maturity. But when it comes to fresh water consumption, it takes over 4,000 gallons of water to market just over 2.2 pounds of beef. In these agricultural and cattle raising areas, agrarians, marketers, and scientists quickly need to find efficient methods for water consumption, yet produce equal or greater amounts of food – a problem. Civilization and the world population need to be mindful that fresh water is only 1 percent, glaciers not included, of water on Earth – a precious commodity. Many countries are stressed for fresh water and may be water dependent on outside sources. The Middle East is extremely high stress, while India is highly stressed for fresh water. The US is classified as medium to high stress in fresh water availability. To civilization's chagrin, 36 countries are facing extremely high stress levels in fresh water availability.

A look at how Singapore, which has the highest water stress level, might reveal some procedures and techniques for water consumption. By very conscientious water management, technological investments, and agreements, Singapore has provided water for an ever-growing population. The small but powerful and free nation has no lakes or aquifers, and the population demand for fresh water far exceeds any indigenous water supplies. First, an agreement with Malaysia provides a good share of fresh water, which is followed by an ingenious system for retaining rainwater. Graywater is dutifully recycled and is supplemented by desalination. Singapore has set an example for the world and countries stressed for fresh water, including the US. Still, the world has over 840 million people who do not have access to safe water and nearly 160 million are drinking surface water.

The amount of food waste carbon dioxide gas estimated by the FAO, Food and Agriculture Organization, is about 3.3 billion tons of carbon dioxide per year. Such an amount is certainly contributory to the greenhouse Earth warming effect. A United Nations projection is that world population will increase to 9.8 billion from the current 7.6 billion by 2050. Food production must increase accordingly, and unless countries and civilization increase efficiency to stop or greatly diminished food and water waste, the world may encounter problems more abysmal than any prior world calamities.

Chapter 31
Climate Change

In several ways, climate change and greenhouse effects cannot be separated from civilization. Simply stated, as civilization increases, the carbon dioxide, CO2, level in the atmosphere and average normal temperatures will increase with time. Presently, the carbon dioxide ratio is 410 ppm, parts per million, but by the end of the twenty-first century, the Earth's atmosphere could be 1,000 ppm, possibly higher. The Earth's population does not need an equilibrium of this ratio. The International Panel on Climate Change predicts about a 4-degree Celsius average temperature change by century's end. Ancient history has provided many millennia for humans to learn and Earth to receive the carbon dioxide effects of increased temperature. However, it is possible the pollutants and carbon dioxide previously dumped into the atmosphere will greatly accelerate the equilibrium to reach 1,000 ppm, causing a temperature rise.

As Homo sapiens are recent to Earth, we need a look at Earth's history for prospective, a look where the Earth has been, and a try for understanding past climates to help predict future ones. While the Quaternary Period was the delivery of the last Ice Age, which we are still in, the Pleistocene Epoch contained the Ice Age from 2.58 million years ago to 11,700 years ago. The Earth's temperature varied enough for 20 cycles of advances and retreats of glaciers. As best we know, Pleistocene temperatures were 5 to 10 degrees Celsius below today's norm, and in the preceding Pliocene Epoch which ran from 5.33 million years ago to 2.58 million years ago, the carbon dioxide atmosphere saturation was 400 ppm, the same as today's saturation.

Our current knowledge shows at least five major ice ages in Earth's history. Humans have only seen the Pleistocene Epoch Ice Age, which is still with us. Civilization is living the good times. Quite remote was the Huronian glaciation that had an interval of 2.4 billion years ago to 2.1 billion years ago, and in all probability, the entire Earth was covered with ice. This oldest and longest lasting ice age occurred during the Siderian and Rhyacian Periods, which lasted from 2.5 to 2.05 billion years ago, including both periods. To Earth's benefit and life to follow this glaciation, molecular oxygen accumulated to cause an oxygen revelation at 2.4 billion years ago. In following Periods and Epochs, complex life could begin with oxygen and stratospheric ozone.

The Cryogenian Ice Age of the Cryogenian Period may have had four ice ages, the first of which probably started 850 million years ago in the early Neoproterozoic Era. The ice ages lasted to about 635 million years ago, and probably made Earth a snowball. At its maximum, the temperature range is estimated at -43 to -25 degrees centigrade, far colder than humans could possibly stand. If scientific estimates are anywhere near correct, the Cryogenian Ice Age lasted, perhaps, for 215 million years, far longer than the human mind can imagine. Paleoanthropology indicates an emergence of Homo sapiens at roughly 300,000 years ago, but behavioral modernity did not occur until about 50,000 years ago near the Upper Paleolithic Age.

Modern-day humans have little to no conception of the gifts with which we have been endowed: oxygen, ozone, livable temperatures, water, the moon, and a stabilized Earth. Yet, "civilization" is too internalized to realize all conditions on Earth are temporary, and that our flagrant, wasteful, and harmful behavior may hasten an age, epoch, or even a period of climate change that is devastating or unbearable for humans.

By looking at a closer time, yet, far removed from the present, we can appreciate Earth's journey to support and build human "civilization." The Permian extinction was at the boundary of the Permian and Triassic Periods, and the recovery was 30 million years into the Triassic Period. While the Permian Period lasted only 47 million years, it contained differences with which humans would have difficulty, besides the end extinctions. Oxygen was a 23 percent of volume or 2 percent higher than the current level, but carbon dioxide was around 900 ppm – not good. Sea levels varied from 60 meters above current levels to 20 meters below, so landmasses of Gondwana would vary considerably. To our good fortune, we do not have that problem today – yet, or repeated.

The Permian extinction was probably a combination of events, rather than a single source. The flood basalt of the Siberian Traps that poured magma for thousands of years accounted for the higher carbon dioxide ratio. Another issue that added to the carbon dioxide level were oceans venting hydrogen sulfide, which destroys ozone. For Earth's life protection, ozone is a necessity against the sun's ultraviolet, life damaging rays.

If we move 184 million years forward in time, the Cretaceous-Paleogene extinction boundary, K-Pg, marks the end time for the Cretaceous Period. The K-Pg was 66 million years ago and also marked the Mesozoic Era, which brought the dinosaurs. Fortunately, the Cretaceous-Paleogene extinction event brought an end to most of the Mesozoic creatures, except the birds. Strong evidence indicates the Earth was impacted by an iridium rich asteroid colliding near Chicxulub, Mexico, since iridium was found at the boundary layer on most of the Earth. Generally, asteroids are richer in iridium than the Earth.

The Cretaceous Period changed the climate to detrimental conditions that many species could not tolerate, including the dinosaurs. After the impact, about 75 percent of all species went extinct, probably due to drastic weather changes. If a lower angle impact occurred, probably, more sulfur and carbon dioxide would have accumulated in the atmosphere. Initially, the sulfur would block sunrays for a few years, whereby temperatures would drop drastically to below freezing, possibly, lasting several years. Lack of photosynthesis disrupted the food chain from top to bottom, causing the deaths of many species – land and marine. It is difficult to determine, since scientific opinions vary, but the K-Pg extinction recovery has a very tenuous estimate of four million years. Yet, the Permian- Triassic extinction recovery has been estimated at 30 million years. In a few years, the carbon dioxide most probably warmed the atmosphere and the Earth.

The evidence of change in the Arctic should give the world's population reason for concern. From decades in the past, concern of Arctic melting was nil to nonexistent. But estimates show a current loss of over 20,000 square miles of Arctic ice every year, and since ice reflects sunlight, heat is absorbed and vast areas of permafrost are melting. The melting, however, releases carbon dioxide, CO2, and methane, CH4, at atmospherically harmful levels. The Pleistocene glaciations from 2.58 million years ago to 11,000 years ago entombed vegetation for the duration, but from the retreat of the last glaciation, permafrost has been melting slowly over thousands of years. Civilization and human activity have caused a more rapid melt rate due to increasingly higher levels of carbon dioxide and methane. The world has reached a cycle point whereby permafrost melting appears logarithmic in its increases – faster warming.

A rough estimate of carbon in permafrost is more than 1.5 trillion tons, considerably more carbon than in the Earth's atmosphere today. Presently, if winters are not refreezing permafrost, then carbon in some form is released continuously, winter included. It is difficult to know the area of permafrost, since much of it is hundreds of feet deep. Our ideas of another glaciation in 100,000 years or carbon dioxide levels not reaching 1,000 ppm until century's end may be just that – ideas. Our accelerated rate of carbon dioxide and methane in the atmosphere is accelerating. Earth has had a good share of ice ages and glaciations. If, for example, we melt the Arctic ice and place enough fresh, warm water into the Atlantic Gulfstream, at some point, the chances are good the Atlantic Gulfstream will stop. Cessation will inevitably bring the world another glaciation or ice age. Probably, the Pleistocene Ice Age was begun by the Atlantic Gulfstream stopping, and, apparently, the world lacked the Gulfstream for thousands of years. Even after a Gulfstream restart, thousands of years were required for recovery.

With the continual Arctic melting, areas and seaways are opening that hereto were unavailable for thousands to millions of years. As the warming trend continues, the elusive and forbidden Northwest Passage may be open for a short time by mid-century, maybe earlier and last longer. Northern and southern routes will be available to the Bearing Sea and beyond. In the long view, this temporary passage may not be to the advantages of the Earth or civilization.

For greed, control, wealth, or power, nations are seeing the open Arctic as an endless possibility to access untapped minerals, oil, gas, and many miles of land advantages. Of course, intrapreneurial enterprise will add pollution and more carbon to the atmosphere. The enterprising efforts are fine, but each nation must be cautious of making waste and leaving it behind, which is a very large a part of civilization's history and societies' self-inflicted wounds. With more carbon dioxide and methane, the next Ice Age looms closer, then, where will civilization be? From evidence of Earth's prehistoric past, which was predominantly contrary to human existence, Homo sapiens are fortunate to have the opportunity to build a civilization – maybe, temporarily.

Chapter 32
SEA LEVELS

As we live in a climate of grace and ease, escaping from the last glaciation of 11,700 years ago, civilization has blissfully become ignorant of where sea levels have been or where they could be. We take our world for granted and erroneously think it will never change, which is forthrightly rejected by science, geology, or prehistoric world studies. Ancient periods or epochs have handed Earth, populated or not, higher and lower sea levels.

The Earth has existed for 4.6 billion years with its ebbs and rises of sea levels being driven by ice ages, glaciations, volcanoes, earthquakes, or tectonic plate movement. Homo Sapiens became existent about 300,000 years ago, but in the last 1,000 years and specifically the last 200 years, humans have had an effect upon the Earth not previously encountered – disproportionate carbon, carbon dioxide, and methane emissions. These elements and gases have been present since near the Earth's formation, but the human intervention of added carbons has interfered with Earth's prolonged cycles. As carbon, especially carbon dioxide and methane, become more concentrated in the atmosphere, heating occurs. There are at least two effects caused by a heated atmosphere: volumetric ocean or sea expansion and glacier melting. If the expansion and melt rates were constant, sea level rise might be more predictable, but due to human's accelerated rate of atmospheric carbon addition, future sea level rise is in the realm of an educated guess. Of concern, the acceleration is accelerating. Secondly, a giga-ton weight change on North or South poles will have some effect on Earth's rotational axis – change, probably for the worst.

The consequences of accelerated Arctic and Antarctic ice melt would be Earth changing and catastrophic for humans. In the worst-case scenario, whereby all ice melts, sea levels could rise well over 200 feet, but such a case is very improbable, however, not impossible. Eons of prehistoric past have not been without ice. Presently, Earth has about five million cubic miles of ice, which would take a few thousand years to melt at the present rate, but some scientists are observing melt rates of Antarctica at three times faster than a decade ago. To our dismay, acceleration must be considered. By some estimates, the year 2100 may see two feet in sea level rise. The rapid melting of Antarctica's ice could push sea levels up faster and higher to, possibly, 10 feet. For a historical time to match Earth's current norm temperature, history must be turned back 125,000 years to an inter-glacial span with sea levels being 10 meters, nearly 22 feet, higher than current levels. Are we going back to matching temperatures and sea levels? We do not know, but the possibility exists.

Predictions on sea level rise varies, and all have some support, yet all predictions will put coastline cities and island countries into some jeopardy by 2100, if not before. Most communities and governments are aware of ice melting and the sea level rise consequences. Regardless, the environment and world warming do not wait for politicians, councils, committees, or governments to act. Some groups are already acting while cities and governments look to raise monies for combating higher sea levels and protection. Unfortunately, there exists no relationships between amounts of political monies spent to climate's effect on civilization, although some politicians erroneously reason otherwise. Money spent by communities can affect limited, temporary environmental protection except for large sea level rises or ice ages. Island nations or communities like Tuvalu, Maldives, or Kiribati could see extinction of their ways of life. The hard realization is that no amount of monies raised will alter the positive or negative effects of nature or sea levels.

Without doubt, Earth's ice is melting and causing higher sea levels with the culprit being high carbon content in the atmosphere. Carbon dioxide and methane are the carriers. Are we beyond criticality of having any way of slowing, stopping, or reversing the Earth's steady temperature climb with resultant sea level rises? According to some scientists, we are precariously close to humans' inability to, at least, slow the temperature increase. World population increase and civilization has contributed greatly to climate change and the sea level dilemma we face. If civilization is to act, carbon emissions must be acted upon immediately, and the US, China, Russia, India, Canada, and Indonesia must lead the world, if human civilization is to persist. To the Earth, sea level changes are nothing new, but for the recency of Homo sapiens, sea level changes can be catastrophic.

Chapter 33
OVERPOPULATION

Recent years have shown some concern of world overpopulation, but as time presses forward, estimates of world population in 2050 are near 10 billion and over 11 billion in 2100. Is the carrying capacity of the world sufficient to accommodate such numbers with a dignified living style? By reviewing the accelerated depletion of resources to support world population now, the concern has amplified considerably on future capacities. An overlooked agricultural fact shows that over produced fields or food sources are not readily renewable. Future overpopulation will need food from sources that are not producing, nullified, destroyed, exhausted, or polluted beyond recovery. Fresh water, fossil fuels, depleted agricultural lands, or living space are a few items that will be in short supply. Of these world assets, fresh water supplies are and will be problems for additional billions of people on the world. As civilizations grow, their sizes become their survival problems. We have created our own life-threatening problems. From several thousand years BCE to our current century, the world population has grown exponentially in the last 500 years, especially since 1900.

The current estimate of world population is over 7.7 billion, but it took about a quarter million years to reach 1.0 billion in the early 1800s. Although there are informed individuals who say the world is not overpopulated, but the rapid depletion rate of Earth's resources indicates otherwise. Agricultural and fresh water have been keyed to population growth to within the recent times, but land resources and fresh water do not renew at a rate to match the population increases. In time, land may renew through nature, artificial nutrients, or added minerals, which adds to pollution and carbon dioxide. If forests are cut for growing fields, photosynthesis, oxygen, and, eventually, ozone are temporarily curtailed. Earth's land area is finite, but the rate of human population is accelerating. Many scientists agree human overpopulation coupled to environmental degradation are the greatest threats to the future, which leads to wars and societal upheavals.

In 1,500 years before CE, plagues, Black Death, starvation, lack of sanitation, and wars kept population growth in check, but the Industrial Revolution by the 18th century fostered a population growth – more laborers. By 1950, science coupled to advanced agricultural techniques such as fertilizer, agrochemicals, better irrigation, and mechanical cultivation brought about greatly increased food production in a given space. The breakthrough was the Green Revolution, and with the revolution, population began increasing due to greater food availability. Common to the Industrial and Green Revolutions were numerous advances in technology.

Throughout history, food increases brought about population increases, and the population increases required agriculturally productive fields to produce more. In requiring overproduction from specified fields, there exists a syndrome of diminishing returns: fields are running short of nutrients and minerals for high-yielding, healthy crops. History has shown a strong correlation of overpopulation to poverty, and that humans will exploit the easiest forests, fields, water, or minerals first and not return to difficult areas until the easy resources are exhausted. The overpopulated world has become environmentally destructive in exploiting difficult or easy areas in order to supply food, minerals, fossil fuels, entertainment, transportation, or defensive materials to ever-expanding cultures. To service these commodities or activities, commercialization has grabbed half the Earth's surfaces, increased emissions 400%, brought to extinction thousands of species, and cleared more than three fourths of rain forests. The US displays no innocence in environmental destruction, since the US represents only a few percent of world population but is responsible for around one quarter of consumables.

The conglomerate of affluent countries are consuming resources at a rate to place warranted concern on Earth's future. The world tends to make comparisons to US behaviors, activities or consumption, and observations indicate US future consumptions will require several worlds. Presently, humanity uses 1.5 planets to satisfy population consumption rates and dispose of waste. Our self-indulgent actions striving toward utopia and urbanization are rapidly propelling the world toward depletion of wild areas and resources. Realization of what humanity has detrimentally caused in a very short period is irrationally disproportionate: vast agricultural land destroyed, atmosphere dangerously polluted, nutrients and minerals depleted, fresh water of lakes and rivers contaminated, forest depleted, and over 800 species brought to extinction. Countries and governments must avoid political rhetoric and intercountry power struggles to universally realize our planet is struggling to support humanities' overpopulated condition. For several decades, there has been little evidence that major areas are countries such as Europe, Japan, China, India, the US, or Indonesia have seriously formed a consortium to recognize the worlds insufficiency to satisfy all humanities ecological withdrawals. Humanity has made little to no serious efforts to check and recognize the dehumanizing results at century's end of 11.0 billion or more in world population. Peoples of the world will face conditions unlike any endured in humanity's trip to civilization. The ratio of people to sustainable Earth's resources is worsening, causing concern for extinctions in the Holocene Epoch.

Some extinctions of the prehistoric past were clearly caused by species failures to adapt. Because the human race's quest for land, ideas of vast control, and ignorance that the Earth can supply all resources forever, humans have overpopulated and placed Earth's renewal capabilities in serious jeopardy. The human race is not adapting and fails to understand the precarious position to which the Earth has been relegated. As, supposedly, the most intelligent species on Earth, we must rapidly gain cognizance of what the human race and overpopulation is doing to our home planet. Without realization, the many peoples of the world are placing themselves on a track of extinction or lives that resemble the Pleistocene Epoch.

Humans are always concerned with costs and expenses, but the world is and will have problems providing fresh water for an infinite number of purposes. The desalination process will convert sea water to fresh water, but the process is very expensive. Several countries are using the desalinization process and are successful. Nuclear power is being used for the conversion, and the price is high. Salt water to fresh water is only an example of what humans are facing. Is the price too high for saving the Earth and humans?

China is the biggest contributor to the world's population, but for 30 years, government policy has been one child per couple. Further, in the Chinese culture, boys are favored in the family; so, in the future, birth rates will decrease. However, the momentum of a large population will still increase the population but at a slowing rate. One problem China will face is an aging population with fewer young people for labor, innovation, and consumption. With fewer males starting families and an increase of non-working elders, the growth rate of producers to the decreasing numbers of consumers will slowly decrease. For China, the decreasing numbers of young people and increasing numbers of elders is hurting producers and manufacturers, even with a slowly growing population. The numbers of the population are one factor, but the population's constituents are another. If the total population continues growing, even at a slow rate, manufacturers will not be able to meet consumer's needs. Although some time will pass before China reaches the population peak, China will begin to experience a below replacement fertility rate.

India is closely following China in overpopulation at 1.33 billion, and in a very few years will have 1.44 billion people, slightly more than China. Worse, a few million Indians are not being counted in Assam that borders Bangladesh, because they are Muslim. Bangladesh is primarily Muslim, and Prime Minister Narendra Modi does not count Muslims in a predominantly Hindu structured state. The Prime Minister sees the Muslims as a latent, potential political problem. Regardless, the Assam Bangladesh – Indians need help and are hungry. Meanwhile, Modi wants the population of Assam to register for Indian citizenship. A task for many, since illiteracy is rampant.

By mid-century, India is expected to reach 1.8 billion and, possibly reach a stabilized population. Currently, nearly 60 billionaires control something short of three fourths of Indian money, which is not invested or circulated in the industry or manufacturing. Such internalization of monies can lead to unemployment, poverty, substandard living conditions, poor or nonexistent social facilities, and inadequate medical facilities, if any.

To feed the population, India is trying to utilize all available land for agriculture, but accomplishment means overutilization of fresh water. Fresh water is an Earth asset, and India is irrigating all available agricultural land, which could cause a couple of environmental problems: other countries need fresh water as well, and water in uncountable amounts in previously un-watered lands adds weight to Earth in a specific point where it was not in prior times. Between the added Indian water weight and China's added weight in countless new buildings, a potential slow change in the Earth's rotational axis is possible.

India is suffering the consequences of excessive population which can lead to dysfunctionality of infrastructure like social facilities, emergency organizations, medical institutions, electrical systems, water supplies, and waste disposal systems. The reasons for India's overpopulation are many. Lack of education is near the forefront of reasons. Uneducated families have difficulty grasping repercussions of overly large families: poverty, starvation, deficient medical care, or diseases that have cures but are not affordable. Contraception is not in their periphery, nor was it wanted. In agrarian countries such as India, large families to the impoverished are an advantage to the family's workforce. More male workers add to income. Impoverished families melded to the land cannot see the long-range repercussions of excessively large families; they see only the possibilities of more workers and enhanced income.

Religions may give reasons for large families. Orthodox or conservative religions may give ideas for no family planning measures. In some religions, women proclaim children are of God's will; so, there is no limit to children in some families. For now, Muslim families produce more than Hindu families, but the future may change this fact, for Hindu families are drawing closer to Muslim reproduction. In India, early marriages are encouraged for poverty, religious, or extended family purposes. Children get married at ages whereby they have no idea of the responsibility required in marriage or child rearing, which, then, requires the aid of already impoverished parents.

India has a population problem that must be solved in the near future. With one third the size of the US, India has roughly four times the population, and over half the people are at the poverty level. Drinking water is a problem in many communities; therefore, many communities schedule drinking water fountains for only a few hours daily. Many women spend hours and miles traveling for potable water, but over one fifth of the diseases are waterborne. Traditional sanitation is limited to only one third of the population. Additionally, many water wells were sunk mindless of sanitation conditions near sewage waste pits.

The US is overpopulated without a doubt. If we look at the population in our sovereignty decoration year of 1776, our population was a few million, probably less than four million. Today the US population is 329 million and growing. If we look at 243 years of growth, the US has increased population at a rate of 1.34 million per year. The rate, however, is increasing to where the US is adding two million people per year. Roughly, half are US newborns, and about half are immigrants. The immigrants are reproducing as well; so, by 2100, the US could have a population that is from 450 million upwards. Can the US handle such a population number? Based on present agricultural production and fresh water consumption, the answer is a clear no. Depending upon the source of statistics, the US has already surpassed a sustainable population by a substantial amount.

Americans are using renewable resources at twice the renewable rate. Looking at the US population in 1970 of 205 million to 329 million in 2019 might explain this fact. In 49 years, the US increased population by 124 million. That period of time indicates a growth rate of 2.53 million per year. From the resources of agriculture, water, minerals, and energy, the US cannot sustain such a rate increase. If all people lived ay America's consumption rates, over four Earths would be required for production of renewable resources, and while energy consumption is nearly equal to previous years on an individual basis our total consumption has increased 25 percent due to population increases.

From the 1700s, the US had vast resources, and for the next 300 years, they appeared unlimited and the country could handle vast numbers of immigrants. Such was true until the years following WWII. In 1900, the US rate of growth was barely noticeable with the population at 76.2 million people. Moving to an anticipated 2020 population of 334.5 million, the US will have added 258.3 million people. While the rate of population growth is increasing, it is difficult to predict a US population in 2100. A low number is 450 million to a high of 600 million people with the real number somewhere between the two.

Looking at resources for support of around 500 million people doesn't look good. For example, western states of millions in population depend greatly upon Lake Mead for fresh water, but it is losing water at two lakes per decade with no real quantity replacement. At status quo, then, the southwest is facing a water shortage, but if millions of people are added, the mighty lake could become a valley. Conservation of Lake Mead is a concern for the entire country, but California, Nevada, and Arizona need to displace the political rhetoric and controlling gestures to face nature's and humanity's diminishment of the lake. If the lake level falls below a surface level of 1,025 feet in elevation, the Department of Interior will need to handle conservation. Conservation would require 1.2 million acre-feet a year to save the lake, which also means some serious conservation of the Colorado River. These are conditions which the US is facing currently, let alone adding 1 to 2 million immigrants per year in view of water consumption versus conservation.

The Central Valley Aquifer loses the equivalent of one Lake Mead per year, but the California Central Valley produces about one quarter of US food from the aquifer. Additionally, the Colorado River Basin furnishes water to about 40 million people in seven southwest states. If the states dependent upon the basin and Lake Mead water cannot continue a conservation and reclamation program in the very near future, the US will have vegetable and fruit shortages commensurate with the water shortage. As the Colorado River emanates from the Rocky Mountains and travels the Grand Canyon, it is tapped to a trickle by the time it enters the sea, and, of course, it is polluted maximally. However, upstream from Lake Mead is Lake Powell and the associated reservoir. Diminished by a growing population, Lake Powell supplies water to 30 million people and irrigation of five million acres of agriculture. Measurements show a decrease of 155 billion gallons per year over the past two decades. In a couple of years, both lakes could lose functions as power and irrigation sources. Once again, politics in states and Congress must be set aside to realize the US population is drawing more water then resources can handle, indicating conservation must move to the forefront of leadership thinking. For the last 100 years, world leaders have had the mindset that resources, including water, were in infinite supply. The world does not possess infinite resources, but for future survival, a world consensus and realization must occur that population growth must stop, decrease over time, and stabilize at a world supportable number.

Chapter 34
SOCIALISM

Throughout human history there have been greater or lesser attempts to establish long-term socialism. The idea from leaders or elite is that everyone receives education, medical care, adequate housing, and equal freedoms by working and contributing a major, measured portion of monies received. Discreetly, socialism will form two classes of people – elite or leaders and the proletariat or commoners. Once socialism becomes entrenched, the lifestyles of the elite remain hidden from the proletariat, who must remain ignorant of government proceedings and operations. Further, it is best the working-class commoners have little or no knowledge of the outside world. Too much knowledge or news from the outside or free world is dangerous to the elite, affluent, and over indulgent leaders.

As socialism precedes, the elite eventually need more of everything, thus, requiring more labor, money, or both from the commoners. The self-indulgent elite may get their socialistic program to last for a while, but additional demands for extravagant government spending stretches production for oil, agriculture, factory products, or exports and will, eventually, reach limits of what the commoners can supply or contribute.

Under socialism, the bureaucratically and incompetently controlled medical system will slowly be tapped of monies for the elite. A single, government-controlled medical system will find quantity, quality, and capability declining with tenure. Within the system, medical personnel have no reason to excel in any manner. There exists no reason for innovation, invention, or improvement, while the status quo, whatever it is, remains the standard.

There are about eight forms of socialism that range from democratic socialism to Soviet Socialist Republic Socialism, which is Communism. Essentially, Communism is socialism backed by a military. Socialism works under the mantra or invocation of each contributing what they can. If an individual wants more or is motivated, the elite encourage more work for more pay – and more contributed to the common good. The system does not encourage innovation or inventiveness. According to the socialist mantra, any profits above replenishment are to be spread equitably among the proletariat. If a worker contributed more, he or she would receive more. What the leaders or elite received will be proportionate to their rank and will certainly be well above worker compensation. For a life of mediocrity, status quo, regularity, and life predictability, socialism may provide a temporary haven, since, inevitably, elite control of proletariat funds will be in deficit for any number of reasons. Within the socialistic structure, the leaders through a quest for control and power do not establish a system of checks and balances. Socialism lasts until the system runs out of proletariat money, and the proletariat begin to grasp their inferior, subjective status, which the elite desires to be infinite.

The social system is touted to providing for those who are unable to work. In every society, including capitalism, there exist those who seek an advantage of the system, and socialism provides an avenue for those that "need" but desire not to work. If socialism allows workers to work at what they enjoy, some labor-intensive areas are sure to be in deficiency. Accordingly, leaders will need to assign labor, much to the chagrin of the laborers. If socialism is true to its mantra, poverty should be eliminated, or if any socialists are in poverty, then all should be in poverty, except, of course, the elite, who know the system is breaking down due to their excessive spending and selfish management techniques. Venezuela is a good example where the country is replete with oil and potential riches that could be derived from those resources leading to free world leadership. Yet, the greed, control, and power quest by a leader and close subordinates have impoverish the people and the country. Venezuela's history of avarice, selfishness, and nationalization has few equals in the world.

Early socialism was pragmatic with its auspices looking to equality of the masses and largely overlooked intellectual, artistic, scientific, and innovativeness for control of the people and their money from labor. Historical beginnings of socialism had a propensity to start with capitalism, since money from rich intrapreneurs was necessary for equal distribution to the proletariat. Socialistic problems are endemic or built into the system. Capitalism will eventually produce rich people who are willing to work, invent, or manufacture to the benefit of others and themselves. Socialism brings its own end – terminal destruction. Even if the rich remained in a downward spiraling socialistic society, they would be driven to mediocrity at best or impoverishment at the worst. Of course, those with wealth would have departed the system long before it's torturous destitute end.

Chapter 35
CHINA

China is the third largest country in the world and the most populous with 1.4 billion people as of 2017. The country does not call itself China but, instead, the People's Republic of China or PRC. While it is ruled by the Communist Party of China, its mantra for the people is authoritarian socialism. Under such a regime, the common people live and endure many restrictions. Freedoms that many countries afford people are either greatly diminished or nonexistent. For example, there are at least 60 restrictions created by the PRC, and with provincial requirements added, people have more restrictions than any other country in the world. The Communist government blocks website substance and busily monitors individual Internet access and subject material. The intrusive government has gone to the expense and trouble of self-censorship mechanisms. For such a large population, the PRC has thousands of people to police and monitor Internet traffic. To remove Internet flexibility, domain name switching or Internet protocol addresses are blocked. With such a government control of the Internet, the capability is nearly useless, or in the worst case, it may be dangerous to use, since anything on the Internet could be interpreted as subversive or anti-government.

While China has a phone system, it seems a certainty local provincial calls are monitored at a high probability. International phone calls are guaranteed to have a high monitor rate. Controversial items to China or the government are blocked from the common people, keeping them more in line with communism. Further freedoms the Chinese people do not enjoy are: assembly, numbers of children, social gatherings, and religion. While the Constitution of the Peoples Republic of China states the fundamental rights of citizens, which alludes to those systematically denied, they are pale or nonexistent compared to criminal rules of prosecution from the state. Symptomatic of the non-applicability of the Constitution is related by China's largest number of imprisoned journalists, who are serving time along with those determined to be Internet and cyber dissidents. Obviously, citizens should be extremely careful using the Internet, gathering in groups, signing anything, communicating abroad – if able – or upholding any kind of government reform. For some time, the PRC has spent time and effort eliminating or neutralizing news, commentary, bulletins, or coverage that is detrimental, adversarial, or criticizes the PRC.

Further allegations against Chinese commoner personnel freedoms carried out by the PRC arise from exterior press reporters and agencies reporting that there are excessive death penalties pronounced, torture, detention without due cause, mandatory abortions, coercion of confessions, and diminishment to fundamental citizen rights. Violent police crackdowns are fairly common, which are followed by mass interment in reeducation camps. Political realignment for over 1.0 million ethnic minorities is a goal of the Xinjing reeducation camps. A preponderance of evidence and reports indicate that General Secretary Xi Jinping and the PRC ruling format are not popular with the Chinese proletariat, considering the plot for punishment to be distributed upon the Chinese people to gain their cooperation, conformity, obedience, and quasi-faithfulness.

Humanitarianism does not qualify as a format or term in the PRC mantra, while slavery is estimated at a little less than 4.0 million people living in those conditions. Incorporated in those conditions are forced labor, child labor, undesirable marriages, and proletariat forced into trafficking. Self-initiated allegiance by the Chinese people shows as a rarity, since positive personal motivation borders nonexistence. However, negative motivation for obedience to the regime exists, as a thousand slave labor prisons and camps are reported. So, as a Chinese commoner, far removed from leadership and the elite, one's hope must be centered on a daily existence subsidized by sufficient food and shelter. The common Chinese person must be happy in mediocrity, live largely in isolation, be not vociferous, be guarded in verbiage, find satisfaction in internal thoughts, and be ever careful of transgressing any government rule. Still, with these criteria fulfilled, the PRC, for no reason, may imprison or apply any number of punishments. There is little wonder why many Chinese are willing to face death or an unbearable punishment to escape China.

While China reports a military budget of well over $150 billion, the real budget is surely much higher. China's goal is to be the supreme world power.

To back the PRC mindset and dominant goals, the Peoples Liberation Army, PLA, has produced the world's largest standing army, containing well over 2.0 million troops. China has become a recognized nuclear weapon power with the will and desire to become a superpower. The US DOD reports the PRC may have 75 nuclear intercontinental missiles and assorted short-range missiles. To project its outside of borders capabilities, China has at least one aircraft carrier, nuclear powered submarines, and ballistic missile submarines. China's airpower capabilities have not been neglected, as the PRC continues building its own assorted fighters as well as acquisitions from Russia. Mixed in the air weapon arsenal are stealth aircraft and combat drones. Far reaching weaponry such as hypersonic and anti-satellite missiles are also in the arsenal. For complementary warfare capability, ground forces have been updated with a modern Type 99 tank with electronic network warfare capabilities. Clearly, the PRC has a distinct purpose to embolden its span of military forces to achieve powers second to none in the world. Efforts, expenditures, and leadership are noteworthy, but if some percentage of these efforts were directed towards humanity and world civility, civilization could show significant gains. China is all consumed with authoritarian socialism under Communism and the subservience of its proletariat population that rights and freedoms of people are not and never will be a government consideration. Unfortunately, the PRC views peoples' rights and freedoms as a hindrance and impedance to socialism's progress.

For many decades, China's thinking has reflected only the elite self-indulgent and aggrandizement thinking with a high disregard to fairness regarding other countries, especially the US. Thoughts and civilization do not center or desire all countries to behave similarly, but there should be a commonality in civilized countries, whereby trade, commerce, cultural exchanges, inter-educational exchanges, travel, and tourism are encouraged. The quality of products should motivate free trade, but greed, followed by self-protection, generates tariffs, a protection tax.

Equal and inter-country fair trade in modern times should be normal, but greed and control exhibited by some countries have inhibited a mode to civility. While China has been directed to fair trade, PRC thinking is having difficulty with the concept due to years of imbalance in its favor. In the long view, it is evident China has no intention of contributing to civilization. Simply, China seeks world supremacy and dominance with the world following the Communist Authoritarian Socialistic mantra. Of course, such world dominance thoughts require the US and other countries to possess and correspondingly enhance offensive and defensive countermeasures. From the actions and subservient ideas for the people, China is a major impedance to civilization on Earth.

China and its leaders primarily think of themselves as an internalized improvement, and to that end, China is pouring more concrete and stacking more steel in buildings, factories, highways, and living complexes than ever before. As a consequence, scientists, geographers, and Earth scientists have noted an eastward north pole drifting of the Earth. A change in the Earth's rotational axis is changing due to a tremendous Chinese weight increase. India's tremendous watering is also adding to the Earth's centroid change, which is not for the better.

Chapter 36
SPACE TRAVEL

Has civilization proven its capability and desire for return travel to the moon and, perhaps, a Mars trip in the near future? Our technology indicates civilization can certainly handle a moon trip, but establishing any kind of present habitat is questionable. For a manned Mars trip, we are close technologically, and to support such a mission, the launching nation must support the effort wholeheartedly from scientists and politicians, which means Congress is most important in the Mars mission. From a US political viewpoint, a Mars mission is not feasible currently. Congress will need to shift its near-total internal intentions to long-term goals of American space travel. Serving the US must return as a priority for Congress, not endless internal affairs and investigations coupled to lengthy, self-indulgent reelection campaigns. For reasons of misdirected goals on internal affairs management, recognition, and self-indulgence, many Congress members have forgotten America and its goals of a great country and civilization. Modern times are showing the US and the world a need for, at the minimum, a human colony on the moon for exploration and raising the human horizon. With an established colony on the moon, assets for further planetary travel may be found and utilized, and the moon offers and excellent launchpad for trips to Mars, which could offer a boon to humankind.

While re-instigating trips and colonization of the moon are important, the real goal is Mars and its possible colonization. The Earth has had an indescribable and lengthy past, 4.65 billion years, and should have several billion years in the future. However, in the future, the duplicity or triplicity of Earthlings having the moon or Mars as assets for alternate colonies, albite heavily modified for human habitation, is rapidly increasing. Earthlings are still in the mode of observing the solar system and the Milky Way galaxy for potential dangers to Earth. The Everest size asteroid at the end of the Cretaceous Period

66 million years ago ended many forms of Earth life, and, unfortunately, there are possibilities of reoccurrence. Given time, the question is when, not if.

Presently, civilization is here and now with little concern of galactic or solar system harm that could infringe on Earth's orbit. For continued survival, civilization must as a joint effort detect and deflect or destroy intercepting celestial bodies. Modern science and astronomy have given world societies limited knowledge of the Earth's solar system and even less of our galaxy; yet, world governing bodies are continually concerned with internal affairs, control, power, or economical trade advantages. More powerful weapons are prominent in many countries for offense or defense. With such leadership thinking, civilized space travel that includes goals for humanity and alternatives for survivals seems unlikely – for now.

Luckily, preclusion of space travel, solar, and galactic knowledge is not complete. Several nations: the UK, US, Russia, China, India, European Union, and the UAE have accomplished or are planning further moon and Mars robot, and soon, manned missions. Accumulated data and knowledge are essential to inform the missions for the future. The beginning nations of space travel and exploration were Russia, US, and China, and are parties to the 1967 Outer Space Treaty, which outlines the moon and space as a province to all mankind. Further amplification was added in the 1979 Moon Agreement that restricted exploitation of moon resources by any single nation. As of 2016, 18 nations had ratified the agreement. In limited pockets of civilization, thought does permeate the political shackles on outside thought and supersedes introverted country dominance ideas.

For space travel, the moon provides an excellent replenishment and launchpad for missions to Mars. Such an environment would be easier under a coordinated, joint mission. However, politics, if allowed, could easily preclude joint missions. If a Mars launch were coordinated and successful, the Mars rewards could be immense. Martian astronomers have guessed at ice water on Mars, and recent rovers have indicated ice water as a fact. Since water, H2O, has components of hydrogen and oxygen, fuel for rockets could be manufactured, assisting deeper solar system travel.

Earth and Mars are the only planets in our solar system that occupy or infringe the habitable zone. During the perihelion portion of Mars's orbit, the planet is inside the habitable zone, but as Mars reaches its semi-major axis in its orbit travel, the planet goes outside of the habitable zone. At any time,

Mars is not habitable, inside or outside the habitable zone. Obviously, space suits and pressurize quarters are requirements for any portion of Mar's orbit. Many reasons are evident for high-quality spacesuits on Mars, but the atmosphere is 96 percent CO2, carbon dioxide, unbreathable for any visiting Earth civilization.

Given time, the probability of Earthlings visiting or establishing Mars habitation is a near certainty. Individual countries or joint efforts may be the means, and in furtherance of peace and Mars exploration activities, all Earth countries should be parties to non-ownership and exploitation treaties of Mars. This treaty or agreement should be similar to the 1979 Moon Agreement. These agreements and treaties are essential and to be in full force before a country or joint effort Mars mission departs Earth. If such treaties are not involved prior to deeper space expiration, our societies are bound to continue Earth's non-civil auspices such as greed, control, power, and war to Mars or beyond. A lack of civil agreements will surely produce failure or catastrophe and not because of space's many adverse elements.

Regardless of agreements or treaties, territorial claims for moon and Mars portions are inevitable. History has proven civilized countries cannot resist opportunities to acquire power, control, and assets. As an example, seven countries originally signed the Antarctic Treaty, which laid aside potential conflict for sovereignty. Antarctica has 5.5 million square miles, and since 1959, 38 countries have signed the treaty. However, several countries have made claims of sovereignty or portions of Antarctica, and, so far, claim validity has not been universally recognized. The analogy for country claims in view of a treaty is a certainty for space traveling countries to the moon or Mars. Simply, the temptation for supremacy or territory is great for country leaders and politicians. Hopefully, Earth civilizations can overcome the desire for celestial aggrandizement, since greed for territorial acquisitions will surely impede space travel.

Chapter 37
International Civil Aviation Organization

The International Civil Aviation Organization, ICAO, is a specialized agency of the United Nations that regulates principles and techniques of international air navigation. Further, the ICAO leads planning and advancement of international air transportation to ascertain safety with orderly, progressive growth.

Currently, there are 195 countries in the world, of which 193 are member countries of the UN, and 192 countries are members of the ICAO. Lichtenstein lacks an international airport. The State of Palestine and the country of Holy See are not members of the UN. The Holy See, Vatican City, is the Roman Catholic church governing body located on Vatican Hill.

The forerunner of the ICAO was the International Commission for Air Navigation, ICAN, which held its first convention in 1903, and by 1906, 27 countries attended in Berlin, Germany. How is it that people were so visionary in the 20th century's very beginning to realize the concept of international flight? Do we still possess such insight and visions of extensive, limitless flight? From the early moments of Homo sapiens' history, humans have an innate propensity to explore and expand horizons beyond the known world. Of course, in ancient prehistory times, civilization was not even a remote concept; yet, early hominid's risked much to improve their lives.

As humanity is on the fringe of, at least, semi-informed space travel, maybe, the ICAO could clone the International Committee for Space Travel, ICSF, for governance of spaceflight. The passage of time and humans' quest for flight beyond the boundaries of Earth will certainly make the term "international" obsolete. For some time, "intergalactic" will not fit for human capabilities, but "inter-solar" might be a future goal and applicable term.

When civilization does possess limited solar system flight capabilities, the need for international flight on Earth will not have diminished. For a stretch of imagination, the equipment for space travel could serve double duty for world international travel in orbital flight. For feasibility, the traveling distance must be great, but the environmental savings would be significant, since carbon emissions would be in space and at the sun's or celestial winds whim. Orbital flight would be from 100 miles and above to avoid orbital decay and take advantage of powerless orbiting speeds in the thousands of miles per hour. Time in orbit would be minimal. The International Space Station, ISS, orbits at 240 miles above the Earth, a non-decaying altitude. International orbital passenger flights could occur between 100 and 200 miles above the Earth.

The idea of ICSF, International Committee for Space Flight, cloned from the ICAO is a giant step and would require monumental efforts and knowledge of orbits, solar system navigation, the moon, Mars, entries, reentries, and rules for space traveling countries. At the minimum, international space traveling agencies need to share schedules, or, possibly, ICSF could have schedules for safety.

Looking at history from the last Apollo 17 lunar landing on December 14, 1972, national and civil priorities changed for reasons of money, politics, and priorities. Nearly 50 years have elapsed since Eugene Cernan left footprints on the moon. Meanwhile, the US and international thinking became more introverted and less interested in space, moon, or Mars endeavors. Greater responsibilities in terms of suborbital or orbital flight became nonexistent for the ICAO or a specialized spinoff of it.

Since the Apollo 17 mission, the Earth and civilization became increasingly concerned with climate warming. The year 1997 brought the Kyoto Protocol, an International Treaty that extended the 1992 UN framework convention climate change. The treaty commits state parties for greenhouse gas emissions reduction and, secondly, acknowledgment that human activity predominantly caused the emissions. One hundred and ninety two parties acknowledged the protocol. Since the ICAO is a specialized agency of the UN, international flights causing exhaust gases, carbon dioxide, and other emissions are an assigned concern to the ICAO.

By 2016, the ICAO was tantamount to Carbon Offsetting and Reduction Scheme for International Aviation, CORSIA. It was determined that 1.0 billion tons of carbon dioxide had been discharged by international passenger and cargo flying. Corporate international flights, which are numerous, also fly under ICAO rules and produce carbon dioxide. The global and ICAO target for emissions reduction is 50 percent by 2050 as compared to 2005. The US, China, and other countries have promised to begin further emissions reductions in 2020, the inception date. The official voluntary start date is 2021, and the mandatory reduction date is 2027. The ICAO has been and will be an enfettered with emissions reduction.

Within UN auspices, the ICAO's prime mission is to regulate rules, principles, and techniques that will facilitate international inter-country flying and long-range oceanic flight. Simply put, international trade, commerce, and expediency would be impeded by a major factor if ICAO signatory countries were non-cooperative and accomplished international flight according to independent rules. If such was the case, safety of long-range flight would be compromised, and air traffic control would be chaotic to non-existent.

While world emissions control and clean up are tantamount to controlling the world warming and climate change, the priorities of ICAO are safety and regulation of international air traffic. Safety through regulation has been and should remain ICAO's reason for existence, not regulating or monitoring carbon dioxide in the airways. Every country, company, corporation, or a mission emitting entity on Earth should take efforts to curb and stop carbon emissions. A regulatory agency, ICAO, for safety of passengers and expediency of flight should not compromise its primary purpose that other agencies can readily and efficiently handle.

The ICAO importance cannot be over emphasized, as it regulates and propagates international civil aviation, which has greatly helped international trade, commerce, and the concepts of civilization. As the Earth stands, any increase in civilized behavior would be a boon to humanity.

Chapter 38
UNITED NATIONS

As an international effort in maintaining and furthering peace, promoting friendly relations, world cooperation, and security, the United Nations, UN, was formed as an intergovernmental organization. WWII was a great promoter with the UN charter being adopted on June 25, 1945, and signed the next day. The functions for the UN have six entities: General Assembly, UN Secretariat, Economic and Social Counsel, Security Counsel, International Court of Justice, and Trusteeship Council.

Opinions have varied on the value and functionality of the UN, but several prominent members have won the Nobel Peace Prize with their efforts. The 1947 General Assembly resolution to partition Palestine made the way for the creation of Israel. Of course, conflict arose, but a UN official, Ralph Bunche, diligently negotiated an armistice to the conflict that could have been quite bloody. When Egyptian President Nasser decided to nationalize the Suez Canal in late 1956, Israel, France, and the United Kingdom invaded Egypt on October 29, 1956, to regain Suez Canal control and remove President Nasser. The Sinai War lasted for eight days with the Egyptians receiving a political victory. Political pressure from the US, Soviet Union, and the United Nations led to withdraw all of invading countries. Of course, the UN was fortified with US and Soviet Union members, but the Sinai War could have affected worldwide trade and commerce.

Once again, in 1967, the Egyptians and Israelis were into a six day war, but while the war lasted only six days, the Suez Canal remained closed until 1975, trapping 15 ships in the canal. While the United Nations and the Security Council had mandates for Suez Canal operations, Egyptian President Muhammed Anwar-el Sadat indicated the mandates would be good for only a few months. Apparently, a lasting operation would be at the goodwill of Egypt and

President Sadat. However, in a speech, Sadat did not want to punish the world, since the Suez Canal is important to world commerce. Regardless of negotiations and speeches, eight years presented a lengthy time for an international, highly utilized shipping canal to be closed, especially since 15 ships of world flags were trapped inside. Without regard, Egypt was hijacking international ships. Surprisingly, this act alone did not instigate war against Egypt. The ships crews were in a survival situation, and in this length of time, the UN could not get the trapped ships freed. Nor, in the eight long years of canal stagnation, could the UN or any country get Egyptians to open the canal. Thankfully, some communication channels were opened, averting a serious international war.

The UN is civilization's attempt to arbitrate for nations with fairness in mind and stand for equality and human rights for member nations. The UN has made a serious attempt at civility with the UN Security Council, which are the five permanent members: France, China, Russia, United Kingdom, and the US. The Security Council specialty niche is peace and security, and for action from the Council, a "yes" vote from all five permanent members is required. On the contrary, a "no" vote from any permanent member nullifies all further actions. When immediate action is necessary, a single nay vote will stop all action. To the UN's downside, an amendment may take months or years appeasing the veto nations – maybe, never.

To expedite UN matters, possibly, a three fifths rule should be proposed for the Security Council. Three conforming votes would pass a "yes" or "no" vote. As in many corporations, institutions, and governments, red tape and layered bureaucracy enfetter expediency, which can be detrimental in the case of a possible war. The inexhaustible regulations and formal rules formed by the UN in an attempt to please everyone are, maybe, politically correct but do not fit an organization that is designed for world peace keeping. Endless debates, discussions, and deliberations without ends or decisions do not lend to expediency when lives are at stake. The UN needs to go by majority; it is not an organization to please everyone and glorify "politically correct"—or, is it?

Why is it the UN budget is comprised of 22 percent US contributions and the next highest contributor is China at 12 percent? Lately, UN has slipped into a format of protecting small interests and countries from big ones like the US. Of course, the UN wants small countries to develop, yet some of these small countries are diametrically opposed to the US while receiving the US money.

The mantra and mandate of peacekeeping with human rights are UN idealistic goals, but the whims and idiosyncrasies of member countries have, at times, blocked UN appropriate actions. Veto powered US and USSR countries have impaired proper UN action. The US participation in the Korean War and the Korean Armistice Agreement on July of 1953 were sanctioned without the USSR. Again, the UN efforts to provide and secure humanitarian relief in Somalia in April 1992 were marked, in part, to an inability to get a cease-fire between the warlords. Supplies for humanitarian purposes were next to impossible to deliver. After casualties in the Battle of Mogadishu, the US withdrew troops, and the situation deteriorated quickly.

The UN purpose reflects the grandeur a civility but is mired down with "politically correct," endless regulations to please endless politicians, crippling veto powers, stagnating debates, and the lack of proper funding. For inter-country skirmishes or outright wars, the criticality of timely decisions, arbitration, or intervention is not a UN weapon. This shortcoming can and has cost lives. The UN was never meant to be a world power or government, but its primary mission is to promote inter-country peace in an expeditious manner but something short of enforcement.

Chapter 39
NEW YORK CITY

New York City is the epitome of civilization's evidence toward progress in the forms of: buildings, transportation, commerce, education, research, arts, advertising, film making, communication, and international relations. Certainly, other countries have their favorite cities as well: London, Paris, Moscow, Beijing, Saigon, New Delhi, Singapore, Chittagong, Mexico City, Buenos Aires, Rio de Janeiro, Tokyo, and many more. Such cities are humanity's attempt at a show of civilization, and each of the cities and others have unique features that advance civilization.

New York City has its own touch on civility, and in some areas, size and quantity are outstanding features. By landmass, New York City has the largest metropolitan area in the world, while the city proper has a population of 8.4 million. The metropolitan statistical area sports a population of 22.7 million. Much of the financial world operates from New York City, and as an example, the New York Stock Exchange, Wall Street, and the NASDAQ exchange are located in lower Manhattan. The largest global center for public equity trading and debt markets has been and remains New York City. While the majority of banking institutions are located in New York City, private equity, mergers, and acquisitions are carried out as well, since Manhattan supplies a plethora of necessary office space.

Higher education is a forte of New York City with an excess of 600,000 students in over 120 higher education institutions, more than any other US city or global cities like Tokyo or London. To further broaden higher education, the City University of New York, CUNY, has over 500,000 students enrolled in 24 institutions throughout all five boroughs. Many smaller, private schools and special-purpose institutions are located within New York City. With the multitude of colleges and universities, research in many disciplines is prevalent: medicine, engineering, biology, anthropology, architecture, mining, amenities, political science, all fields of physics, and many other disciplines.

To further civilization, business, and the millions of working New York commuters, the New York City rapid transit rail system runs 24 hours a day and boasts carrying one third of mass transit users in the US. No other system in the world is larger than the New York City subway system with 472 stations and lengths of routes. The Western Hemisphere has no busier subway system than New York at nearly 1.8 billion passengers in 2015, which at such a rate reliability was a major factor. For convenience, more than half of New Yorkers use public transportation, while more than 90% of the US communities use private transport. The density of New York City forces the transportation issue, but the savings in energy and fuel are tremendous.

As a center for commerce, corporations, finance, banking, and exchanges, air transportation to and from New York City is vital to the world and the US. Incredibly, more than 130 million travelers used John F. Kennedy, Newark, and LaGuardia airports in 2016. LaGuardia is a prime feature for US domestic flights, while John F. Kennedy and Newark support international flying. If civility is to be spread and increased, these airports are most contributive to air transportation and have been for a long time. Long-range flying is a specialty for international airports like John F. Kennedy and Newark, since, for example, a flight from Kennedy Airport to Hong Kong is only 7,000 nautical miles by great circle flying over the north pole. Hong Kong has a new international airport, so the exchanges of commerce, data, and trade could be most facilitative if societies and country civilizations could find agreement and common ground. For the time being, tariffs are recognized as equalizers on trade. Long-range flying can instill or perpetuate exchanges of thought, ideas, plans, and, possibly, cultural understanding.

New York City is the mecca for the media of newspapers, advertising, music, entertainment, publishing, and conglomerates. Seven of eight top advertising agencies have their headquarters in New York, since all the facilities to cover the world are available in New York City. Expediency is at hand. The ethnic presses are available to print 270 newspapers and magazines in more than 40 languages. It would be difficult to beat such a media for spreading civility. The words of peace and civilization are there, but the need for power and control still usurps civility in many world countries.

There are many cities in the world that can vie for populace diversification, but New York City has to be in the running for the most variance. For example, 37 percent of the New York City population is foreign born, and almost every ethnicity is represented in a marked percentage. If there is a language with syntax, it is spoken in New York City, since over 800 languages are spoken in the city. America is a nation of immigrants, and the 12 million Europeans received at Ellis Island can testify to true immigration. In 2012, New York City had a non-Hispanic white population larger than Los Angeles, Chicago, and Houston combined. One might say all races and creeds are represented, except galactic aliens – which may be in dispute.

Chapter 40
LONDON

Without a doubt, London is humanity's effort and contribution to civilization. Whatever the imagination can conjure, a physical representation must exist in London, since the metropolis has been a major city to Europe for 2,000 years. From other societies, global importance is attributed to London, which exudes power, influence, extensive financial capabilities, world commerce, endless arts and entertainment facilities, educational institutions, and a nearly limitless list of disciplines. In banking and world finance, London ranks in the top 12 percent of economic performance in comparison to 300 other cities. London is at least sixth in metropolitan gross domestic products, GDP. In transportation, London competes favorably with any city in the world, national or international. For education in the UK, Europe, or the world, London offers institutions of higher learning on all disciplines known to education.

Diversity describes London with people of all cultures speaking more than 300 languages among more than 8.9 million people. From the early nineteenth century to the early twentieth century, London was the most populous city, and from this rich heritage, there are countless educational and historical edifices and markers to indicate humanity's progress in civilization. The Tower of London to the Natural History Museum are but two of the true markers of humanitarian progress. While marching to civility, Buckingham House was progressively enlarged and glorified from 1762 to 1837. As the population and diversity of London grew, so did the plagues and diseases, and the years of 1848 and 1866 contributed 20,000 deaths to cholera from which the city eventually recovered.

The tenacity toward civilization was certainly demonstrated by Londoners during WWII, as the German Luftwaffe killed over 30,000 Londoners along with destruction of large housing tracts and numerous buildings. The British and London resisted admirably by hosting the 1948 Summer Olympics at

Wembley Stadium, even as London was in deep recuperation. Recovery was strong and steady, and by 2008, London, New York City, and Hong Kong were known as the world's most influential cities. The British and London spirit to recovery and civility are undeniable, even with over 2.9 million or 37 percent of London's population being foreign-born, but an observation indicates these people see themselves as Londoners.

London is most tolerant of all religions, but Christianity is at the highest percentage of over 48 percent. Nearly 21 percent of Londoners have no religion. But, at least, eight religions are present, including over 12 percent Muslim. These religions include: Hindu, Sikh, Muslim, and Jewish communities, which do not war or fight but coexist peacefully. As an example, mosques are in the East London Mosque in Tower Hamlets and are allowed to give the Islamic call to prayer. Hindu communities are in the boroughs of Harrow and Brent, which hosts the Neasden Temple, which is one of Europe's largest Hindu Temples. Most British Jews live in London; however, seven other communities are of Jewish majority. For such a diversity of religions, civility must be a common thread, or religious strife would be a tantamount issue, but it is not. In many Earthly areas, religions cannot coexist without hate, war, or strife. Religious conflicts should not exist, but conflict does exist, even within the same religions. London may have a magic formula, but for the major religions, the predominant factor must be the realization that London is the last step for peace and coexistence. Therefore, major, God fearing efforts are extended and made for peace, a unique feature of London. Should the United Nations be in London?

From the US, many airline and corporate business flights terminate our transit London for business purposes. While other European cities compete for commerce, finance, and banking, London attracts business people from the entire world, and there is reason. With five major business districts: Camden & Islington, Lambeth & and Southwark, the City, Westminster, and Cannery Wharf, there are plenty of possibilities for money exchanges, contracts, and international deals. The London metropolitan area generated $669 billion in 2005, which portends the expediency of business at hand to potential in the future. To handle international business properly, Greater London possesses 27 million square meters of office space. With continuous business dealings, the price of London Metropolitan office space is the highest in the world, and commensurate with office prices, residential property is valued in the trillions of dollars. While price may not be in the criteria for establishing civilization, it certainly establishes value of property where civilized business is conducted, and for business in 2016, London's gross product was $522 billion. London's banking is not isolated to the UK, since London oversees more than 480 banks. This count is more than any other city in the world. As a catalyst to world business, the BBC, a most trusted broadcast network, and numerous national newspapers echo London's worldwide business capabilities.

To transit the world, London has the busiest city airspace in the world, and while London has eight airports, Heathrow, Gatwick, Stansted, and Luton handle the bulk of international travel. Air traffic to and from London to is so heavy that London Control, part of London air traffic control, must assign arrival and departure times for specific points around London and points farther removed. Traffic in foreign country capital cities abide by London control times to avoid congestion.

Helping with transport of business people and Londoners is the London Underground or Tube, which is the oldest metro system in the world with 270 stations. The system dates from 1863. For international business people, the Tube works just fine for transit from one business district to another, since the system handles over 1.0 billion journeys a year.

The above the ground, suburban, Travelcard zones have more than 360 stations to handle travelers and suburbanites traveling from London outbound. Most lines terminate in the center of London with over 180 million people using the 18 exchanges. Once a business traveler understands the London rail system, the rails can accentuate and multiply the business trader's efforts to a higher degree of productivity, especially for those from other countries.

In many circles and societies, education is the key to a civilized world. Education itself is a marker or road to civilization, not civilization itself. But, to be availed to general education and specific disciplines are certainly means to detail, describe, and articulate what constitutes civility in a society or culture. London possesses the institutions of higher learning with the University of London, which has five multi-faculty universities and over 120,000 students. For example, on excellence in learning, the London Business School is a world leading business school with its MBA program ranked second in the world.

The total university and college count in London is 40, not counting foreign universities. The number includes five top medical schools. Currently, the total London student count is 400,000, and, hopefully, the means, knowledge, and skills to establish and maintain civility in the world's cultures will be readily dispensed by these students.

Chapter 41
INDIA

The population of India is 1.4 billion people, and in a short period, India will exceed the population of China. While India is a secular federal republic, it exists as a multilingual, pluralistic, and nearly limitless ethnic society. Remarkably, the per capita income is only $1,500; yet, the literacy rate is nearing 75 percent. In just a few years, India has increased the literacy by a factor of 4.5. Compared to India's early history, the country has a growing, major economy comprised of the world's fastest telecommunication industry, an accelerating automotive industry, information technology services, a space program, entertainment, arts, global pharmaceuticals, and biopharmaceuticals. With the continuing growth rate, India is and will add to world civility.

India is a nuclear weapons state, which calls for an aggressive country to carry and endure additional expenditures. However, the resolve of India is a long- term peace, and for some time, India has been in dispute with Pakistan and China over Kashmir's country sovereignty. Since the August 14, 1947 Pakistan war and split with India, there have been 1965, 1971, and 1999 Indo-Pakistani wars and several skirmishes over Kashmir and Jammu. The partition is not settled yet. Today, India controls 55 percent of Kashmir land and 70 percent of the population. Pakistan controls 30 percent of the Kashmir land, while China controls 15 percent. For further complications, India administers Jammu, the Kashmir Valley, Ladakh, and the Siachen Glacier, while Pakistan administers Azad Kashmir and Gilgit-Baltistan. Finally, China administers the Shaksgam Valley and the Askari Chin region.

On October 31, 2019, Jammu and Kashmir will be re-constituted into union territories of Jammu/Kashmir and Ladakh. All provisions of the Indian Constitution will be applicable. With such a political move, the Pakistanis and Chinese may become increasingly antagonized. Passage of time and the persistence of India, Pakistan, and China to possess nuclear weapons leave humanity little wonder as to the use of these weapons. To a degree, leaders of these countries and others, perceive nuclear weapons as equalizers to sovereignties already possessing such weapons. The game of equalization or one-upmanship in the "humanitarian" nuclear weapon endeavor is not contributory to civilization's progress. Since the dawn of nuclear weapons, the predominant reason for nuclear weapon possession was deterrence, and depending upon points of view, the defensive theory has worked to some degree. Success of deterrence would be hard to measure, but humans still occupy the Earth. For India, Pakistan, China, and other nuclear countries, the idea of nuclear power is a tremendous asset to humanity but nuclear weapons for mutual destruction, until civilization arrives, is not conducive to civil progress nor the future needs of humankind.

Temporarily, India, Pakistan, and China are not warring over disputed territories; however, the country leaders desire more control and power, if not for themselves, then, for following country leaders. Within India, Jammu and Kashmir will become a territory along with portions of Ladakh, but regardless of names or territories brought under the Indian Constitution, the Pakistanis and Chinese have little respect for Indian constitutional proceedings. In this boiling situation, time, temporarily prevails, but civility is in a precarious balance.

While India has relationships with Russia, Israel, and France, it seeks peace, and in time of strife, India has volunteered 100,000 military personnel to 35 United Nation's peacekeeping operations in four continents. However, the early 1960s Chinese nuclear weapons testing and its collusion with Pakistan in the 1965 war gave India the incentive to purchase nuclear weapons for survival. India has no intention of riding in the backwash of other countries, especially those in the nuclear weapon business, and to this end India is developing a defensive ballistic missile system along with a nuclear submarine capability. India has signed a civil nuclear agreement with the US in 2008, and although India was not a party to the Nuclear Non-Proliferation Treaty, it has become the sixth nuclear power state. Similarly, India and Russia have signed cooperative agreements on civilian nuclear energy.

Over the last few years, India has continually improved its economy to where the International Money Fund, IMF, declared in 2017 that the Indian economy was worth $2.6 trillion. India's persistence on world market trading has placed it third in purchasing power. From the early 1990s, the Indian government drastically changed its monetary policies from that of protectionism to a free market system. The protectionist policies were derived from socialism, where internal regulations were isolating the Indian economy and barring free international world trade. Essentially, the change from internal economic thinking to that of external world trade economy brought India to the trading forefront. India has utilized its 514 million workforces well. Ideally and uniquely, India's foreign exchange workforce brought in $70 billion in exchange monies. Other countries do these services but are no match to India. Remarkably, 25 million Indian workers were involved in this foreign trade service. These Indian workers are loyal to India, but have been observed in many countries working limitless trades. Generally, their earned monies are returned to the Indian economy.

Since the late 1980s, over 430 million Indians have departed poverty parameters, and, possibly, by 2030 around 580 million Indians will reach middle-class status. Many of the world's information technologies, IT, are located in India, placing it as the second most favorable outsourcing destination. Predictions from reliable sources form an annualized Indian Gross Domestic Product, GDP, of 8 percent. If this prediction remains true for the next few years, India could be the world's fastest-growing large country economy.

While India is improving economically on world trade, there are domestic humanitarian issues that need correction. The Walk Free Foundation has estimated more than 18 million Indians are living in some form of modern slavery: human trafficking, forced begging, bonded labor, child labor, and many other means. In the early part of the 2000s, child labor was rampant. In this area, corruption is a definite factor, and according to Corruption Perception Index, CPI, India was 78th, score 41, out of 180 countries in 2018, a small improvement from previous years.

While the current population is 1.4 billion, there is only one physician per 2,000 people. At such a ratio, medical supplies can be at a premium, and waiting lines to see a physician can be intolerable, maybe impossible. According to the World Health Organization, WHO, Indian infant death rates are the highest in the world. A regrettable infant rate in 2016 was over 865,000 with a slight improvement in 2017 of slightly over 800,000, but 6.3 million children less than 15 years of age died the same year. By that number, there is one death every few seconds. For children less than five years old, 5.4 million died. To humanity's dismay, most of the deaths were preventable with simple items: clean water, sanitation, electricity, basic medicines, and vaccines. A physician during birth may have prevented complications, but pneumonia, neonatal sepsis, malaria, and diarrhea were the nemeses to the infants' deaths.

With such dire statistics on infant and children less than 15 years old, a need exists to direct commerce funds toward physician procurement that includes obstetricians. The obvious elements are the basics of modern living: clean water, vaccines, medicines, and electricity to operate a clean facility from which physicians can work. Certainly by drastically reducing the child's death rate, the labor force, brain trust, youth, inventiveness, and business climate can be greatly increased for a more productive future India.

While family values are strong in India, child marriages are quite common, especially in rural areas. Regardless of family values, female infanticide, for whatever reasons, is causal to a large ratio in sex discrepancy. In the early 2000s, India had 50 million more males than females. From a humanitarian viewpoint, this obscure idea and procedure should stop. India, or any nation, cannot afford to target infants for death based on gender. For India's future in commerce, technologies, communications, medicine, and pharmaceuticals, the country will need all the youth and brainpower it can muster. Wasting the girls is not the answer.

Chapter 42
Communism

Can civilization inculcated with capitalism survive or exist in a world with socialism or communism? History has slowly indicated communism initially needs capitalism for the production machines, which are run by the working class, laborers, or proletariat. As communism prophesizes, capitalists are comprised of two classes, the owners, bourgeoisie, or elite and the working class, laborers, or proletariat. Conflict between the two classes is largely the basis for societal problems. The elite own the equivalent of production and, therefore, can establish the rules of labor and the wages. Communism desires to correct the conflict of the classes by eliminating the established, profit-based economy with societal ownership of production machines which are under communal control. Many communist philosophers have added, or subtracted, from Karl Marx's theory of communism, but his ideas have been primal and sympathetic to communist/socialistic philosophies. In theory, communism is a single society with no structures of people with communal operated/owned production capabilities. Each member works according to their abilities and receives according to their needs.

Karl Marx is a heavy philosopher and contributor to the theories of communism. His entries into society apparently came from his studies of history, since he was a political scientist, journalist, sociologist, and economist. In his 64 years, Marx advocated his communist philosophies in many places, but spent his remaining years in London, where he died (1818-1883). Much earlier, Marx had met Frederick Engels at a café in Paris, which led to a lifelong friendship, and since they had collateral theories on communism, they collaborated on "The German Ideology" and a more noteworthy work, "Communist Manifesto."

In "Communist Manifesto," a capitalistic democracy receives a critique that focuses on social class causing the bourgeoisie problems on all levels of politics throughout history. Marx and Engels theorize European problems are based on class, which includes the French Revolution, and according to Marx and Engels, class and economics are the driving force of history and our predominant societal conflicts. Material, economics, or both, form the basis of society and are the "superstructure" for society's culture, law, and ideologies.

While the thinking and logic of Marx and Engels appeared sound for a communistic basis, they overlooked some basic human traits that will surface in the bourgeoisie and proletariat classes of people. In the communal ownership of material and production, eventually, hard decisions must be made for success and continuation, and from history and economics communal or committee decisions are not always in the best interest or production. Communal decisions could be time-consuming or inaccurate, not assets to efficiency or production.

From psychological studies, groups, committees, or gatherings of people will eventually produce a leader or a form of leadership. Generally, it is not a human trait to remain stagnant, neutral, or conform to a laissez-faire approach to life for an indefinite period. Some members of the bourgeoisie and proletariat classes will eventually seek some form of improvement. For Marx's and Engel's theory of classes causing strife within a capitalistic realm, it appears a paradox that proletariat and bourgeoisie "classes" of communism were dissatisfied with status quo.

Before the Soviet Union was dissolved on December 26, 1991, Lithuania, Estonia, and Latvia were dissatisfied with a communist rule. Pressure on Mikhail Gorbachev was dissension from those soon to be republics for independence and international recognition. Apparently, Gorbachev was pressured into allowing elections with a multi-party system, which seems contrary to a truly communistic, one party system. With elections, the system would create a presidency for the Soviet Union, but a process of democratization began that would destabilize communist dominion and dissolve the Soviet Union, something Lenin and Stalin could not envision.

By the early 1990s, Gorbachev's power as the president was weakening, and the unsuccessful coup in August of 1991 by hard-liner communists determined a Soviet Union downfall fate. Gorbachev resigned after the coup; whereby party power was diminished in Soviet Union Presidency. With the hard-communist coup failure and Gorbachev's resignation, the powerful Central Committee dissolved. The hard-communist view diminished with the Central Committee's disappearance and President Gorbachev's resignation.

Before 1991, the Baltic states were already displaying dissension in the communist ranks with independence from the Soviet Union in the minds of Baltic state leaders. Somehow, secretive thoughts were running in the minds of bourgeoisie and proletariat class people for some time, an indication the good-life communist propaganda had not infiltrated the minds of rational thinking people.

The US was carefully watching the Soviet Union communist breakup, which was hard to believe after a long head to head Cold War with nuclear weapons in the balance. From 1947 to the Soviet Union dissolution on December 26, 1991, the US performed an alert status with strategic bombers and missiles for the prolonged unpredictability of communist, world power seeking leaders. Finally, the "no class" communist country was overcome by people who wanted freedom, independence, and the exercise of abilities to exceed the status quo established by the bourgeoisie. The high theories of no class utopia by Karl Marx was finally usurped by thinking, rational humans.

During the 1991 Soviet Union dissolution, George W. Bush, the US 43rd President, used the organic approach: let the Soviet Union dissolve on its own. Meanwhile, Ukraine and Belarus along with the Baltic states of Estonia, Latvia, and Lithuania were seeking independence and their own international recognition. From long-time communism, many countries, including the US were suspicious of inculcated, hidden communism. However, James Baker, Secretary of State, proposed five capitalistic democratic rules that the countries must accept for international, independent recognition. The rules espoused: each country must respect international law and obligations, support democracy and the rules of law, recognize existing borders, observe preservation of human rights and rights of national minorities, and follow self-determination using democratic principles. It is quite obvious these rules are directly contrary to communistic, no class, no ownership, and pay for work only ideas of status quo living.

In what appeared as a communist Soviet Union stopgap, Boris Yeltsin, first President of Russian Federation, met with leaders of Ukraine and Belarus in Breast and established the Commonwealth of Independent states, CIS, which made the countries independent, free of communism, and self-determined. The formation of the CIS signaled the demise of the Soviet Union.

As the Soviet Union unfolded from within, the cause predominately lies in proletariat disgruntlement with their lowly status quo assignments. Under the communist regime, the closest communist action to an incentive or a positive reinforcement was: more work produces more pay. The workers or proletariat cannot look forward or hope for life or position improvement, let alone become a free, part or whole, intrapreneurial owner of any production machine. Worse, the workers' children can expect nothing more. The sentence for life is a rewardless working career and existence.

Homo sapiens have an innate nature to survive and improve the conditions in which they are living, or we would not have survived to modern times. Communism has overlooked the human desire to innovate, invent, or improve conditions to ensure survivability. The human genus is not suited to handle an indefinite status quo. Therefore, humans are generally repulsed at lengthy or lifetime status quo jobs. Human brains are not suited to communistic classless, no thought existences. There is no goal or reward for exceptional behavior. Achievement is nonexistent, and, therefore, reward is without basis.

Chapter 43
AIR TRANSPORTATION

From 1903, airplanes, aviation, and air transportation have advanced by phenomenal leaps. As airplanes advanced in capacity, speed, reliability, and safety, the airline industry advanced civilization by a remarkable degree. To arrive at the current airline industry capabilities, which carried 4.1 billion passengers on a global basis in 2017, history provided the necessary sciences, organizations, airports, navigation capabilities, and rules for safety for all aspects of passenger carrying aviation.

Initially, science, engineering, and aerodynamics afforded the momentum to provide aircraft that could exceed 100 knots and carry, maybe, three passengers in some degree of safety. WWI propelled aircraft to greater speeds, but for the most part, the fighter aircraft were the recipients of speed increases. Passenger capacity was in the beginning stages after the war. Advanced thinking had not disappeared, however, when the Ford Trimotor made its first flight on August 2, 1926, it was the largest civil aircraft in America. The corrugated aluminum construction, safety of three engines, size, and Ford name were favorites with passengers, and, of course, the newly forming airlines took a particular notice. The 5-AT, Tin Goose entered air service in 1928. The top speed was more than 130 MPH. Horse carriages, trains, or cars could not match such a speed. Civilization was on the airway for exponential growth. Certainly, more advanced aircraft were to follow.

For speed of expanding economy and rapid movement of people and freight, the transportation industry, including some fledgling aircraft manufacturers, began designing aircraft with capabilities exceeding the Ford Tri motor, tin goose. In this tentative and beginning business was the Douglas Aircraft company, which was founded in 1921 by Donald Wills Douglas Senior. Later, in 1967, the company merged with MacDonald Aircraft, which became MacDonald Douglas. Later, in 1997 MacDonald Douglas merged with Boeing.

In the beginning of the 1930s, Trans World Airlines, TWA, 1930-2001, wanted an aircraft that could approach 1,000 miles of range and a speed of near 200 miles per hour. By July of 1933, Donald Douglas Aircraft had designed and aircraft to meet the specifications, and on July 1, 1933, the DC-1 flew with a passenger capacity of 12. TWA accepted the DC-1 on September 15, 1933, with the added modification of a couple more seats and more powerful engines. While the DC-1 tenure was short, TWA ordered 20 more with modifications, which became the DC-2. The DC-1 was sold in 1938, and in December 1, 1940, Iberia Airlines had a subcontractor operator, Negron, make a forced landing in Malaga, Spain, which damaged the only DC-1 beyond repair.

The DC-2 made its first flight on May 11, 1934, and was a successful airplane that evolved to the DC-3, which flew on December 17, 1935, and became the famous, reliable, safe, most utilitarian airliner and transport aircraft ever produced. Through the late 1930s, 1940s, and 1950s, most airlines had a few DC-3s. For the military, the C-47 transport is the DC-3 in military uniform and configuration. DC-3s are still flying, which states a remarkable track record.

If ever there was an aircraft or airliner that accelerated the world's movement toward civilization, the DC-3 is the foremost contender. The DC-3 was prominent in the US where it flew all domestic routes. Unfortunately, many smaller towns in the US are no longer served by airlines that utilized the DC-3. For smaller towns, terminals had to be built and maintained. Monies had gone elsewhere, with consolidation to large metropolitan airports as the chief competitor. Less people live in the country or smaller towns, as larger cities are favored.

By flying to smaller towns, domestic and foreign, the DC-3, DC-2, Fokker Trimotor, and Ford Trimotor helped growth in societies, cultures, and also many foreign countries. Earlier, the DC-2s, Fokkers, and Ford Trimotors helped remote villages and towns with transportation, communication, and commerce. Later, from 1935 and on, the DC-3 greatly assisted foreign villages and towns to become worthy of map recognition. The DC-3 could cross the continental US and made worldwide flight possible.

The 1930s provided the US government evidence that air traffic was increasing and that safety, economy, and regulations were going to be necessary ingredients for present and rapidly growing air traffic. In 1940, President Franklin Roosevelt wisely decided that two agencies should be formed to establish control, safety, and rulemaking for the rapidly advancing air traffic commerce.

First, the Civil Aeronautics Administration, CAA, was formed to establish an air traffic control system, rules for safety, and airway systems. The undertaking and establishing required planning and money. Air traffic control towers are expensive and controllers need training and certification. Even in the 1940s, air traffic control centers needed to be established to monitor and control airplanes on designated airways, and, of course, air traffic control did not have radar. Control was by two-way radio for altitude assignments and estimates to published airway points. With the advent of radar, control and safety improved greatly. However, navigation by satellites and aircraft flight management systems, FMS, have eliminated much of the two-way radio communication – advancements to civilization.

Simultaneously, President Roosevelt took steps to establish the Civil Aeronautics Board, CAB, which was to instill safety, established rulemaking, conduct accident investigation, and form economic regulations for the airlines. 1956 brought the midair collision of a United Airlines DC-7 and a TWA Super Constellation, L-1049, over the Grand Canyon; whereby, in 1958 the CAA became the Federal Aviation Agency, FAA. The Civil Aeronautics Board continued but safety rulemaking moved to the FAA. Since the military was flying heavily, the FAA became responsible for civil and military aircraft to utilize commonality in air navigation and air traffic control.

Within the US airways, control towers, and air traffic control centers, all people working within the system are under FAA rules and must be certified to do their specialties. All pilots and air traffic controllers are certified by the FAA, not state governments. For each position an air traffic controller works, a certification is held. All airline pilots and nearly all corporate pilots hold the top rating, Airline Transport Pilot, ATP. The corporate jobs do not require the ATP, but the corporations, insurance companies, and many foreign countries make the requirement.

To assist airlines with expediency, the airport infrastructure must be configured to maximize utility and minimize ground time. Such an accomplishment requires on the spot refueling, coordinated freight and baggage handling, galley and laboratory servicing, expeditious crew changeovers, if necessary, minor repairs addressed, and flight plans posted within the air traffic control system. Addressing economy of operations requires the airport infrastructure to expeditiously handle these tasks. Several entities may be involved; so, coordination and communication are of great importance. For expeditious handling of air traffic over Pacific Ocean waters, international waters, the ICAO, International Civil Aviation Organization, has granted the FAA authority to control airways and air traffic.

Each foreign country or state must act similarly, if international air traffic is to be advantageous to civilization. To a large degree, countries have abided by ICAO rules for expeditious and safe international air travel. Of course, there are exceptions, and they are the no personal freedom Communist countries.

From the standpoint of efficient domestic and international travel, can we say that our current "civilization" has advanced more than if there were no air travel?

Chapter 44
OCEAN SHIPPING

From the middle 1850s or before, ocean shipping of every cargo imaginable to worldwide ports has helped build societies, cultures, and beginning civilizations to an immeasurable degree. Oceanic shipping occurs in six groups: cargo, container, tanker, reefer, multi-purpose, or dry bulk, bulk cargo, container, and tanker are of concern here. In any category, more weight by the ton or bulk cargo can be moved more efficiently than other modes of transport. Other modes are efficient in their own realm. Trains are quite effective for rapid transport of cargo from fixed point to fixed point. Trucking can move fairly large loads rapidly and can vary the route or make changes as required. Airfreight is by far the fastest mode but is limited to 100,000 pounds to, maybe, 400,000 pounds. While ocean shipping is the slowest mode, freight, bulk cargo, or oil may range from 100,000 dead weight of tons to 550,000 dead weight tons, DWT, not pounds. Such weight can be moved efficiently around the world in weeks or months at speeds of 25 knots or so.

Cargo ships are built for specific purposes and to serve humanity in expeditious manners. For example, to navigate the Saint Lawrence Seaway, a freighter cannot exceed 28,000 DWT. Other dimensions also apply for the seaway passage. Transporting cargo from the Atlantic Ocean to the Great Lakes and metropolitan areas can only be accomplished by the smaller freighter.

Around the world many countries which border oceans or seas have modified or are building ports to handle Chinamax carriers of 400,000 DWT with their 1,180 feet length. Port design can expedite entry, loading or unloading, and departure. Such ports assuredly have cranes for loading and unloading. A port with multiple births can handle cargo ships in hours as opposed to days of yesteryears. Larger cargo ships handled by efficient ground crews will shorten times and increase economy for themselves and the port city – economy of scale.

Ancient countries that excelled in their strides toward civilization like Rome, Greece, or Egypt developed cargo ships for inter-countries trade, whereby, cultures not only exchanged goods, wares, or food but information and learning. Ancient Grecian cargo vessels controlled a large portion of world trade. Their cargo vessels continually improved and moved from slow oarsmen power to sailing power. The Greeks primary material for vessel building was wood, which allowed construction expediency with expert woodworkers already at hand. By 500 to 400 years BC, craftsmen could manage boats from 100 to 150 feet, and the passage of 150 years or so produced skills that allowed the Greeks to build ships close to 500 tons. Commensurate with their ship-building skills, the Greeks began to expand their trading routes to include the Mediterranean Sea, Egypt, and the Far East. As the Greeks' trade routes increased, their economies increased as well.

In many ways, ancient Maritime countries were thinking ahead of their time. Laws of countries that traded and exchanged cargo, goods, art, or wares mutually respected the laws of sailing, docking, loading or unloading cargoes, and exchanges of monies. With mutual respect, maritime countries could prosper.

In the mid-1950s, container ships began to increase efficiency in carrying capacity. Conformity was a must for cargo containers to drastically reduce loading and unloading times. The primary size of the containers is 20'x8'x8' or 40'x8'x8' which allows container ships and ports with cranes to standardize and not waste time resizing for a variance of loads. The revolutionary container shipping method increased economy of scale again by reducing port times from days to hours for all logistics, including refueling. Recent container ships are a matching size for oil tankers, since size and capacity are conducive to economy. The evolution of container shipping has progressed to around 90 percent of non-bulk cargo on a worldwide trade basis.

Commensurate with container ship development, major shipping ports have adapted to handle multiple ships simultaneously in less time by utilizing standard container handling equipment. The port of Singapore has a long-standing record of commercial and military ship handling, and the early 2000s showed it as the busiest port in the world. The same timeframe recorded the top 20 busiest world ports handled a little short of half the world's total container traffic. When a 350,000 DWT to over 500,000 DWT container ship docks at a capable port, civilization, no matter where, is about to get a gargantuan boost in economy and growth.

While the oil tanker does not produce oil, it certainly delivers the oil, producing energy to promote civilization and culture over the entire world. Oil tankers are either huge and designed to carry crude oil from points of extraction to refineries or are smaller tankers that carry refined products to distribution points for consumer use.

Much as cargo and container ships developed, the early oil tankers actually carried oil in wooden barrels, which, of course, leaked. Fortunately, the sale driven tanker progressed to something resembling a modern tanker but lacked modern amenities. Initially, single hull tankers were used, but oil expands and fumes were problems. Around 1883, tankers were produced with multiple holds that spanned the tankers beam and length, and by subdividing the holds, sloshing and tanker capsizing could be avoided. Time improved tanker construction that incorporated safety features, and by the early 1900s, Royal Dutch Petroleum emerged with ownership of over thirty steam driven oil tankers.

Until 1956 and the Suez Canal closure by Egypt, tankers were built to fit the canal. However, ship owners were conscious of cargo and container ship economies derived from size. Therefore, oil tankers were manufactured to sizes of 500,000 DWT and larger; for example, the "Seawise Giant" weighs more than 560,000 DWT. The size economy surpassed canal fit.

Clear sailing for all takers was not to be. Certainly, WWII was terrible for oil tankers of any flag, and the US east coast deep sands can give evidence of U-boat torpedoing. Oil residue from sunken tankers is still there. Later, in 1989 the "Exxon Valdez" accident in the Alaska did nothing to help conversations about oil tankers of any size. The "Exxon Valdez" oil spill was an environmental disaster whereby the US subsequently required all tankers that operate in US ports to have full double hulls. Naturally, the double hull tanker does not solve all oil spillage problems, but the extra hull adds a tremendous amount of protection against bottom collision caused spills. For the added weight, an oil tanker is more costly in manufacture due to the double hull, which is not required for passenger liners, cargo ships or container ships.

From ancient times to the present, transport of mega cargo loads, container, or oil has proven cost-effective by ocean shipping. Many ship cargoes increase in profitability as the cargoes increase in mass or size. 400,000 DWT to 500,000 DWT of the ships traveling at 25 knots may not seem economical, but economy in size realization is sometimes difficult. Further economy is gained by only a few hours of unloading and loading, thus releasing the ship for further economies.

Has ocean shipping pushed humans toward improving cultures and civilization? Ancient cultures to modern times with humans' attempt at civilization give a resounding affirmative answer.

Chapter 45
DISEASES OF CIVILIZATION

In the Earth's formative years, asteroids, meteors, and comets most assuredly brought microbes and bacteria to Earth. So, some of our microscopic friends or enemies may have been on or in Earth's composition since the Pre-Cambrian beginning, which was 4.6 billion years ago. However, at the Precambrian close some 544 million years ago, a mass extinction occurred. Possibly, some microbes or bacteria crossed into the Cambrian Period. The possibility exists, but sure knowledge is elusive. The Earth and the current lifeforms are most assuredly living with microbes, bacteria, and viruses now. As Earth's life forms progressed, especially Homo sapiens, the bacteria needed targets, and Homo sapiens were on the eligibility list. Early humans had discovered survival and procurement for food increased by living and hunting in groups, the formative times for culture, society, disease, and, much later, attempts at civilization.

The clusters are grouping in clans or cultures also brought about the contagiousness of bacteria or viruses from which Homo sapiens may or may not have possessed immunity – probably not. In our early days, a Smilodon, saber tooth tiger, or a big woolly mammoth can see to your demise. Smilodon populator, one of the biggest cats of all times, could weigh nearly 900 pounds, but, fortunately, the Smilodon became extinct about 10,000 years ago. Unfortunately, our cohabitants, the bacteria, viruses, and microbes did not see extinction.

From 300,000 years ago and the probable coexistence of Neanderthal and Cro-Magnon, the two humanoid species undoubtedly dealt with diseases and afflictions. Moving forward to a few thousand years BC, the Egyptians had to deal with bacteria and virus problems as their culture preferred groups for pyramid building, transportation, and food production. The progress toward civilization brought health and disease problems as well.

The fourteenth century CE saw the Black Death, bubonic plague, sweep through Asia, Europe, and Africa, causing the death of around 50 million people. European deaths may have been as high as 60 percent, but exact numbers are impossible. Many Europeans died a horrible death from contagion. The side effects of such high death rates were revolts from lack of understanding, more crime, persecution, and a greater need for welfare. While the Black Death was worst in the fourteenth century CE, a probable precedence for the bubonic plague was the Justinian plague or the Mediterranean plague in the sixth century CE that affected Constantinople, Antioch, Alexandria, Pelusium, Rome, Carthage, Marseille, and Trier at the least.

The nineteenth century CE was still a time of no cure for bubonic plague where an outbreak occurred in the Yunnan Province of China in 1855. Via boat shipping trade with flea infested rats aboard, the plague quickly spread from China to India. Twelve million people died, with India having 10 million deaths alone. The World Health Organization, WHO, declared the pandemic was still active until 1960 when casualties dropped to 200 per year. The world's third bubonic plague pandemic is still lurking about. Antibiotics are effective against the plague, but from an initial diagnosis, the plague victim has only 10 days to live.

Unfortunately, there are many diseases awaiting humankind, and civilization either causes the diseases or exacerbates them. Although many countries have sanitary conditions, poor sanitation does exist throughout the world: contaminated water, primitive living conditions, and little or no sanitation. Within civilization, tight groups inevitably form, which are catalytic to contagious diseases, and from history of primitive times to the present, scientists and those in the medical profession were generally in a quandary for cures as new diseases appeared. For example, polio or poliomyelitis was unknown before the twentieth century, although a Louisiana outbreak of polio occurred in 1841. A half century passed before Boston recorded polio cases in 1893. The polio virus had set in by 1907, with New York City reporting around 2,500 cases. The virus needed close living groups to advance its paralyzing calling card. The virus was elusive from 1907 to 1955, when Doctor Jonas Salk produced an inactivated vaccine. In 1961, Doctor Albert Sabin developed an attenuated vaccine. However, polio is still with us because children are not inoculated for whatever reason.

Modern society considers itself and citizens to be quite advanced, but we still have ancient diseases with us. We are living with past enemies such as: bubonic plague, swine flu, polio, leprosy, tuberculosis, Chagas disease (parasite), hookworm (parasitic roundworm), smallpox, acute respiratory syndrome, avian influenza, and Ebola.

Homo sapiens have an innate desire to survive and advance in all fields of endeavor, or we wouldn't be present on Earth now. And advancement for humans arrived through innovation a few thousand years ago in the form of agriculture, and as humans advanced, technology allowed fewer laborers to produce more food for more people. As we have advanced, society has produced sedentary office workers and those that labor to keep society running, including agricultural efforts and production.

Modern society has produced diseases of civilization, which to a large degree did not exist thousands of years ago. We pretty much know the causes of modern maladies, which may be part of a metabolic syndrome. As the office cadre are promoted to higher offices, physical exertion declines to near zero, maybe—pushing elevator buttons, weight increases, lungs lose efficiency, metabolism decreases, blood pressure increases, while the heart and other organs get weaker. For our modern diseases, then, we have: ischemic heart disease, strokes, respiratory problems, pulmonary problems, diabetes, cirrhosis, and Alzheimer's disease. Modern society has produced an abundance of food which is mostly high in fat, cholesterol, sugar, and preservatives of unknown origins. Typically, too much food is consumed while exercise or labor remains near zero. Fortunately, most countries do not have the problems of food overconsumption that is prevalent in the US.

In many respects, human bodies are still back a few millennia. Certainly, we have advanced scientifically and technologically, but our bodies may need the exercise of years past hunting and gathering. The prehistoric times required Homo sapiens to store energy for survival hunting. Rest and stored energy, fat, were part of life. Dealing with woolly mammoths and saber tooth tigers was not an easy task and should have been avoided, if possible. However, clan survival was a primary duty of hunters.

Homo sapiens bones from ancient times did not show arthritis until the advanced ages. Such bones are a rarity, but bone injuries were frequent, a part of ancient life. Humans require vitamin D, and our ancient ancestors were assured of an adequate supply from the sun, but modern humans may be deficient in vitamin D, since many of us work for hours in covered, air-conditioned offices. Modern humans also love a thick, rich cut of meat, but the fat content is far greater for world animals now compared to prehistoric animals. To our chagrin, the excessive fat on cattle now doesn't help with heart disease, which prehistoric humans, probably, did not experience.

Modern times and our dietary habits coupled to a lack of exercise has placed humans in serious overweight conditions – 30 pounds. Obesity has produced far too many deaths per year, which is coupled to billions in expenses. Is our lifestyle bringing us to extinction?

Chapter 46
OPINIONS

In many world countries and areas, civilization alludes leadership thought. Sometimes the status quo or the here and now situations are difficult to surpass. Tradition established by forefathers, religious dogma, antiquated government procedures, laws, or foundless historical ideas may be difficult, not impossible, to overcome. Thoughts to the world's future must transcend greed, control, power, and subservience of parts or all of humanity. The world has seen these attitudes in many past skirmishes and wars of control, and, most recently, WWI and WWII. The world and societies suffered greatly from introverted control and power thinking from leaders of the past German, Japanese, and Italians countries. Currently, the world must contend with misbehaving leaders and dictators of Iran, Iraq, Venezuela, North Korea, and China, while Russia, Syria, Turkey, and the Middle East must be carefully observed.

With undo world attention on potential skirmishes or wars for control, difficulties arise in saving or producing fresh water, cleaning the oceans of societal refuse, preserving forests for oxygen and ozone, controlling or managing the refuse of humanitarian living, and mitigating the destructive power of nuclear weapons that many countries possess. Nuclear weapon countries see the need of possession to counter another country's potential power takeover. Still, humanity is in the business of mutually assured destruction, MAD.

Closed countries, like North Korea, China, Russia, Iran, and Venezuela, prevent true exchanges of humanitarian ideas, since they are in the business of controlling, monitoring, enslaving, imprisoning, or spying on their people and others with the motives of control and power in their leaders' minds. While leaders of these countries have mindsets of rule, control, power, and no civilized thoughts of freedom, other leaders have thoughts of equal rights, futuristic ideas, inventiveness, and efforts for better lives through free market capitalism.

There is little doubt that humans through carbon and carbon dioxide emissions are, at least, catalytic to world warming over many decades of expediently and cheaply disposing of human, manufacturing, and atomic wastes. Many years ago, our brain trusts assured society that the oceans could handle and dissolve what wastes we dumped into the waters. Some years have passed, and any thoughts to dissuade oceanic dumping have disappeared in light of monetary motives. Cultures want convenience and profitability. Seaside cultures are only recently realizing the consequences of ocean dumping, since the carnages of yesteryears are now washing ashore and blatantly reminding people of their ancestors' ignorant, erroneous thinking about waste disposal.

While current societies may not be aware of oncoming fresh water shortages, fresh water lakes, especially the Great Lakes, have been trashed and used as waste disposals for years. At best efforts of recovery, it is seriously doubtful the Great Lakes will ever return to pre-settlement and pre-manufacturing days. We have and are trashing the freshwater Great Lakes for expediency and profitability. At the expense of fresh water, societies are working themselves to achieve civilization.

Many countries, including the US, freely use underground aquifers when times of drought occur. Food from crops and thoughts of profitability were the driving motives for large draws from underground aquifers. However, most aquifers took millions of years to form, and the waters drawn from them will take time for replacement, if it ever is replaced. Our past, shortsighted thinking is now forcing some sacrifices in the agricultural world. Crops needing less water were arbitrary in the past, but, presently, they are getting more consideration with less water. Undoubtedly, people are not going to give up favorite foods, like wheat, alfalfa, corn, rice, cotton, which are water intensive crops. Sorghum is a very efficient water crop and drought tolerant, and it may be more prevalent in the future as a cereal. Scientists and agrarians are working on genetically modifying plants to improve their ability to find water. If predictions are correct, the next 40 years will produce another 2.5 billion people to feed. Crop production will have to double with watering efficiency and conservation reaching efficiency levels unknown today. From scientists, it takes one liter of water to produce one calorie of food. So, for the 2.5 billion annual feeding increase, a 55 percent increase of additional water will be required per year. Such a water requirement is, at least, twice that of today, which under current conditions is not feasible.

Possibly, to measure auspices of civility in the world, a look at countries possessing nuclear weapons could be noteworthy. First, a question of what nuclear weapons do? Primarily, such weapons destroy anything within a large radius, which is proportionate to the size of weapon. The weapon is capable of destroying an organized society and leaves an aftermath of deadly radiation that can last for years, preventing repopulation and rebuilding of a culture. Secondly, the question arises of why countries see a need to possess nuclear weapons. Almost all countries possessing weapons will respond in eloquent diplomatic dogma that defense is the reason, and in some cases, this idea is true. A good offense is the best defense bespeaks the rationale for weapons. But, heavily, internally controlled Communist states bear watching from the external free world. These countries tolerate the free world and wait for opportunities to insert control in weak, indecisive, or third-world countries, and are backed by nuclear and sophisticated conventional weapons. Once control has been established, a dare of defiance becomes apparent. Would it be that Venezuela is tantamount in Communist observance?

The relationship of countries that need the most observation for aggressiveness are the same countries with little to no personal freedoms, great internal censorship, internal and external spying, and must follow a communist dictator. Russia, China, and North Korea fill the criteria quite well. Additionally, there is a Chinese dictator wanting world entrenchment and power. Trust in these countries must be measured carefully with the resultant being very near zero. Their deceit, lies, spying, and subterfuge over history warrants no credibility. While diplomacy or international negotiations are the peaceful and correct ideas, any outcome with these communist powers must be carefully measured by mutual established criteria for the future. Regrettably, these countries only understand and respect the "big stick," which gives reason for free countries to possess nuclear weapons – more setbacks for civilization.

In view of prolonged, greedy, controlling, dictatorial countries, world civilization presents a near zero probability. Although world organizations, UN and NATO, strive for peaceful intercountry relations, history indicates negotiations with communist regimes nearly always produce futility, near or long term. If an agreement is reached, Communist prevalence in the dictatorial countries will find reason for breach.

The countries that currently possess nuclear weapons to a significant degree are: United States, Russia, United Kingdom, France, China, India, Pakistan, North Korea, and Israel. The numbers of weapons range from several thousand to slightly less than 100, but any are significant.

In all probability and for millennia, nuclear weapons will exist on the world, but for strides forward in civility, world important negotiations should not be caused by or backed by the possibilities of weapon use. How close to reality is such a proposition? For the present, the idea eludes reality, but the future always holds promise.

About the Author

Bob Barr's flying career spread over 51 years and produced over 21,100 hours of combined military and civil flying. His military career encompassed several aircraft, but the B-52 and OV-10 were primary for 309 combat missions in South East Asia and Vietnam. Combat flying produced a Distinguished Flying Cross, DFC, and 14 Air Medals. For noncombat military activity, Bob was awarded assorted other metals. Bob either instructed or evaluated in the B-52, OV-10, or C-131 aircraft.

In the civilian world, Bob did some freelance flight instruction and had CFI/II/ME, certified flight instructor, instrument instructor, and multi-engine certificates. Primarily, Bob was a pilot, senior captain, and chief pilot for the world's largest oil service company that had Dick Cheney as the CEO for five years.

This type of corporate flying looks at the world as a destination. Fortune 500 companies insist on airline transport pilot, ATP, certificates with type ratings for its pilots and a good educational background. With the ATP, Bob has BS, MA, and MBA degrees.

www.ingramcontent.com/pod-product-compliance
Lightning Source LLC
Chambersburg PA
CBHW070657250726
48662CB00001B/167